THE POWER
OF
SEXUAL SURRENDER

offers hope to husbands and wives who wish to achieve a mature and satisfying marriage. This enlightening book contains the answers to fears and questions most women have been unable or unwilling to express.

Are men responsible for frigidity in women? Are some women "born frigid" and others not? Is the woman, by her glandular and physiological makeup, automatically accorded the smaller share of sexual pleasure and fulfillment? Can frigidity be "cured" by hormones or by surgical and mechanical means?

Dr. Robinson examines and dispels these and other long-standing myths, confronts women with the true psychological nature of their problem, and shows how frigidity can be turned to fulfillment through self-knowledge and the power of sexual surrender.

Other SIGNET Marriage Manuals

THE POWER OF SEXUAL SURRENDER

by Marie N. Robinson, M.D.

A SIGNET BOOK from
NEW AMERICAN LIBRARY
TIMES MIRROR

SIGNET TRADEMARK REG. U.S. PAT. OFF. AND FOREIGN COUNTRIES
REGISTERED TRADEMARK—MARCA REGISTRADA
HECHO EN CHICAGO, U.S.A.

SIGNET, SIGNET CLASSICS, MENTOR AND PLUME BOOKS
are published by The New American Library, Inc.,
1301 Avenue of the Americas, New York, New York 10019

FIRST PRINTING, APRIL, 1962

PRINTED IN THE UNITED STATES OF AMERICA

PREFACE

I believe that the problem of sexual frigidity in women is one of the gravest problems of our times. Over 40 per cent of married women suffer from it in one or another of its degrees or forms. And their suffering, emotionally and physically, is very real indeed.

Those who are most closely related to the frigid woman— husband and children—suffer too. This is so because frigidity is an expression of neurosis, a disturbance of the unconscious life of the individual destructive to personal relationships. No matter how much she may consciously wish to, the frigid woman cannot protect her loved ones from the effects of her problem. Thus figidity constitutes a major danger of the stability of marriage and to the health and happiness of every member of the individual family.

Despite its extent and seriousness, women who suffer from frigidity generally know very little about their problem. They do not know its nature or its causes nor how or where to find help for it. No adequate book for the lay reader, nor any popular magazine article that indicates a real way out, has yet been written on this enormously important subject. The problem has been surrounded by silence, and this has engendered ignorance, misinformation, and has fostered feelings of helplessness and hopelessness in the suffering individual.

I have written this book to break this unhealthy silence, to bring to the individual woman what science knows about frigidity, to show her that, no matter how much she may have despaired, her problem can almost certainly be resolved.

MARIE ROBINSON, M.D.

November 1, 1958
New York, N.Y.

CONTENTS

SECTION III
The Fear of Love—Case Histories

SECTION IV
The Bridge to Womanhood

Chapter 1

PARADISE LOST

Happiness between men and women has never had such a radiant outlook as it has in this decade. Perhaps for the first time in the history of man the two sexes find themselves in a position to explore together the infinitely varied and rich potentialities of real love.

I am not being a blind optimist in making such a statement. In my profession as a psychiatrist I see enough of daily misery and destructive misunderstanding between men and women to keep a healthy skepticism very much alive in my mind about all human relationships, particularly those that depend for their continued existence, at least in part, on sexual love.

I can make such a statement about the potentialities of modern love for one reason—that women today have, beyond the shadow of any doubt, achieved complete equality with men. Above all, this equality can be observed as fully operative in the realm of love, sexual love. In the past thirty-odd years, and particularly in the last ten, the taboos, ignorance, and misunderstanding which had obscured our visions for centuries and prevented any real knowledge of feminine sexuality have been washed away.

We have been through a sexual revolution of major proportions. In the course of that revolution we have learned, through science, not hearsay, the real facts. We know now that woman has the same need for passion, the same capacity for sexual response that man has. We know that, down to the last detail, she is the equal and fitting companion for all his possible raptures, can know with her entire body and mind and can share in vivid companionship the delighted storms of sexual love that in the recent past were considered to be exclusively his province.

Few, however, realize how recent and how revolutionary this view of womankind actually is. The image of Victorian woman, that sexually frozen, emotionally withdrawn vestal virgin, has faded quickly from our minds. It is important, for many reasons, to recall her, however, if only briefly. She dominated our whole view of womankind up to the beginning of the 1920's. By taking a quick look at her we can see how far we have come in so short a time. And we can see why the prospect for love has, in our time, brightened so considerably.

The prevailing attitude toward woman and her sexuality throughout the nineteenth century and up to the end of World War I was that sex, as we understand it today, did not exist for her. This belief was held by virtually everybody, and it is nowhere more clearly stated than by the medical authorities of that era. Thus Acton, a leading medical specialist in the functions of reproduction, whose views were widely influential, wrote: "The majority of women (happily for society) are not very much troubled with sexual feeling of any kind." He also stated that people who believed differently were making a "a vile aspersion" against women. Two other doctors of the time agreed completely (and presumably after checking their facts). Fehling held that any appearance of sexual feeling in a young girl in love was "pathological." And Windschied stated that if a female showed any innate or spontaneous sexual attributes "there is abnormality."

These men were not crackpots. They were reputable and distinguished. This was the "scientific" view of the matter, and it was shared by most people, men and women alike. It throws into clear relief the potentialities of the present. Woman's new and revolutionary self-awareness, her knowledge gained in the past thirty-odd years that without guilt or inhibition she may function in an atmosphere of total equality with men and eager acceptance by them, makes the past seem like a nightmare. It is as though man and woman had emerged from a long, long journey through a dreary jungle full of fear and shame to the verge of a paradisal valley where they actually may live, as in the fairy tales, happily ever after.

But now we come to the tragic flaw in this picture. For,

though the possibilities lie before them, millions of women find they must stay on the verge of, never enter, the paradisal valley. They find themselves, in an age where true womanhood is highly valued, sexually frigid.

What does sexual frigidity mean? I shall explain the matter in greater detail later, of course, but I can give a preliminary, working definition now. Sexual frigidity is the inability to enjoy physical love to the limits of its potentiality. The frigid woman is, to a greater or lesser degree, blocked in her sensual capacities. Generally she cannot experience orgasm. If she has one at all it is weak and unsatisfying. Many frigid women, however, not only do not have any orgasm but may also lack the capacity to feel even the beginnings of sexual excitement. To some the sexual act is painful.

The frigid woman has learned to fear physical love, to run from it, and this fear has profound repercussions on her relationships with men. The reasons for her fear are hidden from her, are locked in her unconscious mind. Consciously she may wish, above all things, to achieve real closeness with her husband, to give and receive the greatest of all mutual joys between man and woman, sexual gratification. But she has not the capacity to receive this joy. It is beyond her will and control. It is as if she had a million dollars and could not spend a cent of it; as if she were surrounded by the finest foods and must starve. The very fact of the new equality she has won makes her problem even more humiliating, bitterer, more frustrating.

In my fifteen years as a psychiatrist and psychoanalyst I have treated many, many women who have come to me in despair because of their partial or total inability to enjoy the sexual part of their marriage and because of the repercussions from this inability. I and hundreds of other psychiatrists have been fortunate in helping many of them to overcome their difficulties. We have found that before a woman can be expected to take full responsibility for reaching true sexual maturity she must really know all about herself, her sex, and her problem. Then and only then has she the material in hand to start growing up, in all pleasure, to her full feminine stature.

If a woman is willing to work in all seriousness with a psychiatrist there is little question that she can be helped to overcome her sexual difficulty. The information she receives, the insights she obtains into the conditions which have kept her from experiencing real love can sweep away her ignorance, her misunderstandings, her irrational fears.

Her experience with the psychiatrist may help her husband, too, for with his wife's consent the therapist will often see him for periodic discussions. These talks help him to understand her problem, to see deeply into the nature of his wife and therefore of all womankind. This knowledge allows the husband to be of direct help in effecting his wife's release from the immobilizing grip of her frigidity. It helps him to be patient where he might have been irritable, tender when he might have been importunate; it keeps him from the major error of believing that he is to blame for her underlying condition and thus complicating the relationship by becoming defensive, as one unjustly accused would become— indeed, *should*.

The question then arises as to whether the kind of information a woman and her husband may receive during her therapy can also be helpful in book form.

I have given much thought to this question and have had many consultations with my psychiatric colleagues about it. We have come to the positive conclusion that a book on this subject can be of direct benefit to all women suffering from sexual frigidity.

I will go even further and say that the facts about frigidity that I present here—its origins, its causes, and its cures— *must* be known by every woman with a sexual problem if she wishes to be cured.

Frigidity is always rooted in incomplete knowledge gained in childhood and adolescence. We are not, as I have pointed out, far from the Victorian age. Any woman of thirty or more had, in all probability, parents who were reared in the traditions of Victorianism, which denied the sexuality of woman, connived with every available force to deny it, repress it, stop it at its source. These efforts were extraordinarily successful. And, too, any woman now in her twenties probably had parents who were deeply affected by the equally mindless and vicious protest against Victorianism which characterized this country from, roughly, 1920 to 1930— the period we now call the Roaring Twenties or the Jazz Age.

This era, too, was full of destructive misinformation about sex and love. A program of sexual promiscuity for women was openly advocated and found far too many adherents in the younger generation after World War I. The moral climate created in the Jazz Age was alien to the very nature of truly feminine love. It led to serious sexual conflicts in millions of individuals, and these conflicts were duly visited on their offspring.

This book then, I firmly believe, can help the individual to undo the early harm caused by improper upbringing. I have tried to design it in such a manner that a woman who reads it completely may achieve a deep understanding of frigidity, an understanding that can lead to a profound inner change, a complete reversal of those attitudes that are always at the root of frigidity.

I have designed it, too, to be read by the husband of the woman who suffers from frigidity. It goes without saying that the success of his marriage is dependent on the resolution of her problem. He can help greatly to ensure this resolution by fully informing himself of the nature of the problem and by discovering the most helpful role he can play during her recovery.

But the problem of frigidity does not concern only the married. Thus I have also aimed this book at those young people who are about to enter their first love experience. We have found that this first experience can be of vast importance for the further emotional growth of the individual and of the relationship upon which she has embarked. Young women who find they have problems in the sexual sphere may be spared years of misery if they are given a real understanding of the matter in the beginning. Many of my patients, had they been given an insight into the nature of their difficulties at the start, might have avoided the inevitable and innumerable poor choices and often disastrous decisions which are so characteristic of the woman suffering from a sexual problem.

Since I have designed this book to answer the needs of a specific audience I should like to ask you to read it through and not skip around trying to find the material that seems to apply directly to you or to someone close to you. For, if you follow me as I go, you will see that frigidity is not a single, simple, local symptom. It is a complicated and profound problem involving many factors and having profound consequences. One *can* grasp the nature of this problem, understand it, and cure it. To do so, however, you must have very specific and complete knowledge of it in all its complexity. It may take all your powers to master this complexity. To do so, however, will be more than merely worth while. It can be the first great step toward real love, upon whose threshold you have tarried already far too long.

Before we advance into the subject itself, I should like to dispose of a few widely held and thoroughly incorrect notions about frigidity. I do this to clear away some of the underbrush which can impede those of you who are seriously seeking a resolution of the problem.

In the first place, let us look at this problem of a woman's sexual "responsibility," as it has been recently called. Much has been written about it and much of what I have read is pure nonsense, based on a sort of mechanical conception of what love is and of what the act of love means. I fear that such books encourage women who have deeply rooted sexual difficulties to approach the problem from the wrong direction and before they properly understand the real nature of their difficulties. Such an approach leads them to attempt abortive "solutions" which can only further discourage and disillusion them. The basic error here is in trying to make the individual woman "responsible" without giving her any real information about her condition.

The fact is that no woman who suffers from frigidity consciously desires to. Nor can she be, for a single second, held accountable for the fact that the problem developed. The word "blame" cannot by any stretch of the imagination be used in connection with her problem. I strongly urge you to let that point sink deeply into your heart and mind.

How could it possibly be that you had any responsibility in the matter? This problem always develops in childhood or even infancy. It is partly a product of early family and historical influences over which you had not the slightest control, and it is partly a matter of the biological heritage of all women everywhere. And you certainly can't be held responsible for that.

Here is the attitude I have found most helpful to take toward this matter of sexual responsibility: You are not responsible for having developed a difficulty; you are not responsible for the existence of your frigidity any more than the stutterer is responsible for his stutter. However, once you realize it is a problem, that it is having repercussions on you and those dear to you, you are responsible for finding out everything you can about the problem and then, on the basis on this information, taking whatever action is necessary.

I have already mentioned another important misconception about frigidity and should like to go into it a bit further now. I have said that it is highly unlikely that the husband of a frigid woman is responsible for her frigidity problem. I can't emphasize that enough. Of course if he is impotent, was when his wife married him and has continued to be, she might have a case. But true sexual impotency in the male is quite rare. Even, however, if he were truly impotent, the fact remains that this particular woman did marry him

—we have found that when a woman marries an inadequate man she has done so because she, all unknown to herself, was deeply afraid of true male virility.

In saying the husband is rarely if ever to blame for a frigidity problem I am running counter to a vast body of information that has been published; in the 1930's in particular, book after book appeared, each showing conclusively that a happily married sexual life depended on the male's skill in arousing the woman. In such books the husband was instructed to manipulate or caress her for X minutes in Y number of erotic zones. By then, presumably, she would have reached such a state of excitement that true sexual satisfaction could not possibly fail her. Any failure of a woman to respond adequately in the marital bed was always supposed to be due to faulty technique on the husband's part.

This is simply not true. Caressing or manipulating the genitalia or secondary erotic zones of certain types of frigid women would only result in exacerbated nerves or in a condition of inwardly screaming protest. In other types, caressing might give temporary satisfaction but in the long run could really be harmful from the psychological standpoint, deepen or encourage immature methods of gratification.

In short, while a husband, through tenderness and understanding, may help a woman face the true nature of her problem, he is never responsible for the *existence* of her frigity and cannot, through any mechanical means, get her over it.

I might add that neither can any man other than her husband.

Another misconception about frigidity: Women who suffer from a greater or lesser degree of frigidity often come to believe that there is something wrong with them glandularly. Through a misunderstanding of something they've read or heard, they get the idea that somewhere, somehow, there is a drug that will cure them. A gynecologist I know tells me that he has at least three women a week ask him to give them hormones to step up their sexual responses. On the basis of his statement I have checked with several other gynecologists and also with five obstetricians. They all tell me that the request for hormonal injections from women is a daily constant.

Let me say here that frigidity is rarely a problem of glandular malfunction. Much work has now been done in this area and, unless your case is relatively unusual, you may rest assured that your problem is basically a personal and psychological one.

How can I be so certain of that last statement? Because real frigidity reacts to psychological treatment; it can generally be cured in a psychiatrist's office without the use of any drugs whatsoever.

If you reply: "Well, perhaps the mind has caused a glandular shutdown in women with a frigidity problem," we would answer: "Even if that were true the mind would still be the 'cause,' and a real cure can be effected only by getting at the cause."

A far more serious misunderstanding of the nature of true feminine sexuality and of the nature of frigidity is shown by the following case, told to me by a psychiatric colleague.

A pretty young woman came to him stating that she had been unable to have sexual satisfaction in intercourse. She had told her physician of her problem two years previously. He had examined her and told her that her clitoris was too far from her vagina. He informed her that this biological fact made it impossible for her husband to contact the clitoris with his penis during intercourse and that this was causing her frigidity. The physician advised an operation which would bring the clitoris and the vagina closer together, thus allowing the penis to contact the clitoris during intercourse.

The woman, in all good faith and with a laudable desire to be a good wife, had gone through with this grotesque surgical procedure. After the operation, when she was able to have intercourse again, it had apparently worked. For two months she had had orgasms during intercourse. Then slowly but surely her ability to respond disappeared. Within three months she had become totally frigid.

Nothing could be more mistaken than such an approach to the solution of a sexual problem in a woman. In the first place, surgery performed on the genitalia of a woman who is already sexually disturbed can cause profound shock to her psychologically, deepen her disturbance immeasurably—such was the case with this woman, my colleague told me. Second, the fact that the clitoris and not the vagina is responsive is a form of frigidity in itself. Even if this maddeningly ridiculous operation had worked in the manner the physician had hoped, it would only have perpetuated a situation that was in itself, psychologically speaking, pathological.

The psychiatrist did not have an easy time with this patient. The traumatic experience caused by the operation and its failure had taken a toll, and it took several months for her to recover from the psychological effects. But she was a determined young woman.

When she became convinced that the solution of her problem lay in discovering the hidden misunderstandings about sexuality that had occurred earlier in her life, she set about this task with a will. In a relatively short time, through insight and understanding, by getting the entire picture of frigidity and its meaning, she began to undo the Gordian knot that even the surgeon's keen knife could not cut. At the root of her problem lay a totally hidden fear of pregnancy which she was able to face and dispense with. Today she has two children and, according to my colleague, is not only sexually normal but very happy in her marriage.

Let me make myself absolutely clear, even at the risk of repeating myself. Frigidity is in the vast majority of cases, essentially a psychological problem. The *only* way it can be approached with any hope of resolving it is through the mind, by understanding it. Anybody who tells you differently is, to put it plainly and simply, wrong. And, if you have a real frigidity problem and try to ascribe other than psychological reasons for it (such as that your husband is the cause of it), you are doing your cause (that of getting over the problem) a grave disservice.

When I say that the problem of frigidity is a psychological one I am not overstating the case; I am, to simplify matters, rather understating it. The greatest contribution of psychiatry in the past sixty years has been the discovery of the central importance of sexuality in the development of the individual. Dr. Therese Benedek in her classic work, *Psychosexual Functions in Women,* states the whole matter succinctly when she says: "... the sexual drive ... is the axis around which the organization of the personality takes place."

When all goes well in the development of the young girl, both her personality and her sexual passions will flower, she will achieve a beautiful and integrated maturity. But if, as so often happens, thwarting or blighting experiences take place, the development of her personality and her sexuality will be frozen at their sources, and maturity will remain a never-never land whose very existence she will come to doubt.

If she wishes to resume her growth she must be fearless, she must find out and face the events that blocked her growth, the misunderstandings and ignorance that prevent her from reaping the rewards of true womanhood. She must insist, deep within herself, on achieving that true and passional relatedness with her man for which there is neither simulacrum nor substitute in woman's journey through life.

The bridge to emotional and sexual maturity is built of

many facts—hard, scientific facts. Master these facts, gain
information on this subject, and you can pass from a land
of bitter deprivation to the richness that is your due, your
heritage. It is waiting for you on the other side of your fear.

Chapter 2

THE NORMAL ORGASM

The first thing I am going to do on this, so to speak, journey with you is to give you a view of your destination. I am going to describe an orgasm to you. I am going to describe it in detail.

We occasionally do this in psychiatry when dealing with a frigidity problem, and sometimes it has astonishing results. I have seen women who, after hearing for the first time a complete description from an authoritative and objective person of what to expect of themselves in the act of love, almost immediately win through to the sensual goal they had been deprived of.

On one occasion a patient of mine, who over a period of months had worked through a rather severe frigidity problem, detailed to her younger sister the wonderful sexual experience she was now able to have. The younger sister had been married only two months and had not once reached sexual climax. She had seriously contemplated consulting a psychiatrist about her "problem." The very night her older sister described true orgasm to her she was able to achieve her own first complete satisfaction with her husband.

However, my chief motive in approaching the subject of frigidity by describing the normal orgasm is not to try to bring about a sudden or miraculous cure. In cases where such a sudden release of mature sexuality is achieved and thaw comes like a sudden spring, the frigidity proplem is generally, even though it may appear to be deep-seated, a superficial one, lightly rooted in the personality.

The real reason I start with the orgasm is that a picture of the normal is an absolute necessity if you are to understand deviations from it with any real clarity. It is a truism that in order to understand illness in the body it is first necessary to understand health. Every doctor knows this and so do his teachers, for in medical school he first learns, through classes in anatomy and physiology, the structure and functions of the healthy body.

I think you will understand frigidity more thoroughly if we pursue the same technique here, first describing the genital anatomy of woman and from there proceeding to a description of the normal orgasm, what it is, where it is located, its function in the healthy man and woman, and other pertinent material.

Despite the wide dissemination of sexual information in our time, many women often show an astonishing ignorance of their own genital region and of the character and meaning of sexual response, including orgasm. I have had patients who did not know that they possessed a clitoris, others who make no distinction between their urethra and their vagina; some have not known of the existence of the uterus as a separate organ, and some, in confusion about their uniquely feminine secretions, have believed that women can have a seminal ejaculation as men do. Perhaps most of the readers of this book will have no such misinformation, but nevertheless I feel it is wise to review the simple facts pertaining to the feminine genitalia.

Before making a detailed description of woman's sexual apparatus, I should like to make a preliminary observation which can help you to understand the sexual nature of woman. It is this: that while women are capable of having true sexual gratification in the same sense and with the same intensity as men, they have one important difference in their responses. The man, when he is aroused, feels the sexual desire directly in his genitals. A woman's first sexual sensations are not usually genital but are felt over her entire body, on her skin surfaces, everywhere; *this* is followed by sexual excitation in her genitals, and this is an important fact for both men and women to understand. Ignorance of this fact has given rise to many misunderstandings between the sexes, for of course it makes the woman somewhat slower in reaching the moment when she is ready for intercourse than the man is. It *must* be taken into consideration by both parties to an act of love.

A woman's genital apparatus is both internal and external. The external genitalia are called the vulva when they
are referred to all together. The most obvious part of the
vulva is the part we called the major (or sometimes outer)
lips, which enfold the rest of the genitalia. If these lips
are parted we see two smaller lips; these are called the
minor lips and have a very high degree of sexual responsiveness. Even in books for laymen the Latin words are
often used for these two organs: *labia majora* and *labia
minora,* which mean, simply enough, the major lips and
the minor lips.

The labia majora also contain within their folds the rest
of the external genital structure of woman. Here we find
the clitoris, the vestibule, and the urethra, or opening to the
bladder.

The clitoris is by far the most important and most widely misunderstood part of the external genitalia. It lies immediately above the top fold of the labia minora and is a
little piece of tissue slightly less thick than a pencil. This
organ is enormously important to the whole psychological
and sexual development of the individual woman. It is often
called the "homologue of the male penis," and this simply
means that in the embryo the cells which form the penis in
the male are the same cells which form the clitoris in the
female. Thus the two organs have the same cellular deri-
vation.

The clitoris, like the male penis, is made up of erectile
tissue, and when a woman is sexually excited it becomes
erect in the same manner that the penis does. It also has
a head and a foreskin covering it, and the head of the
clitoris, at least in children and adolescents, is generally extremely sensitive to stimulation. In the fully mature female
this sensitivity often diminishes, giving way to the vagina as
the primary source of the greatest sexual pleasure. However, many women who become fully mature sexually maintain much of the original sexual responsiveness of the clitoris.

The remainder of the external genitalia is contained within the vestibule. This is the entrance proper to the vagina
and is very susceptible to sexual excitation. The vestibule
lies between the minor lips and is directly beneath the clitoris. It contains the hymen, the urethral opening, and the
opening of the glands of Bartholin.

The hymen is generally referred to as the maidenhead. It
is a thin membrane which partly covers the entrance to the
vagina. There is no direct sexual sensation on the hymen,

and sometimes pain is experienced when it is perforated, usually during the first intercourse, although the hymen can be broken by an accident in childhood, through the insertion of surgical instruments, etc. Because of the pain associated with its perforation and the stories that a young girl often hears about this pain, it can be a source of much anxiety to her and condition her attitude toward sex in general.

The glands of Bartholin are of great importance to the act of love. These glands discharge a thin colorless mucus in sexual excitation, and this lubricates the vaginal opening and canal during intercourse. The amount of secretion varies greatly with each individual. Sexual frigidity often affects these glands adversely, causing the secretions to be inadequate or nonexistent. However, the amount of secretion will also vary rather dramatically at times in the individual who has no basic sexual blocking, and therefore the glands of Bartholin cannot be taken as a final criterion of sexual adequacy or inadequacy.

And now we come to the most important part of a woman's anatomical sexual equipment: the vagina. This is a passageway of some three to three and a half inches which extends from the vestibule on the outside of the cervix, which is the bottom end of the uterus. The vagina is, of course, the canal which accepts the penis, and it may interest you to know that in Latin the word literally means "a sheath for a sword." The sexual act in its purest form expresses the essential passivity associated with women and the aggressiveness of the male, the actor and the acted upon. The Romans understood this basic difference at least linguistically.

It may have surprised you to learn of the relatively short length of the vagina. The tissue of its walls are extremely elastic, however, and not only can it contain a penis of virtually any thickness or length, but it can stretch enough to allow the newborn infant to pass through it. The penis presses against the cervical end of the uterus, which may be forced upward until the penis gains full entrance. Contact with the soft tissue of the cervix is a source of great pleasure for the male, and the pressure can be an equal pleasure for the woman.

The vaginal walls are lined with a soft skin, not unlike mucous membrane, but it does not secrete as mucous tissue will. A secretion is, however, released from the cervix, and this also helps to lubricate the vaginal canal during intercourse.

I have said that the vagina is the most important part of a woman's sexual equipment. This is so because it is within the vagina that the orgasm of the truly mature woman takes place. Upon it and within it she receives the greatest sensual pleasure that it is possible for a woman to experience.

And this brings us to the subject of orgasm. I think you will undertand it more fully if I describe it in the context of the sexual experience as a whole.

The sexual instinct in both men and women is marvelously complex. When it is unencumbered by neurosis it gives color, shape, brightness, charm, vividness, and direction to the entire personality, and the mechanisms by which it operates encompass both body and mind.

Desire can be cut off in a woman either in response to a touch or by some act, sight, or thought which she has been exposed to. One of the chief things to which a woman responds is a cumulative tenderness expressed in words or in acts.

Whatever the stimulus, however, the brain receives the signal and, through the nervous system, sends out preparatory reactions throughout the body. The response of men to stimuli perceived by the brain as sexual is amazingly fast; some men arrive at full sexual preparedness for intercourse within three seconds—that is, their penis becomes fully erect and ready to enter the vagina within that time. Women react, on the whole, somewhat more slowly, though full preparation for intercourse, under the best of conditions, is often only a matter of a few more seconds than the man's.

As the sexual excitement increases, tremendous changes go on throughout the body, changes that might frighten you if they occurred under other circumstances.

The pulse rate goes up astonishingly. There are records of its reaching 150 and more as the individual approaches and then reaches the sexual climax. Such pulse rates generally occur, in health, only in athletes who are performing prodigious tasks of speed or endurance.

The blood pressure, too, goes up precipitately. In a matter of a few seconds it can rise well over 100 points. Breathing also becomes much deeper and swifter. With the approach of orgasm the breathing becomes interrupted; inspiration comes in forced gasps and expiration occurs with a heavy collapse of the lungs. It is as though the sexually excited person had been in a race.

As the sexual act continues there is a general shortage of oxygen throughout the body, which accounts for the unusual breathing. This gives rise to a tortured expression on the face, as if the person were undergoing severe pain. This fact has been observed by Kinsey in his famous study of female sexuality, and I quote here an interesting paragraph on the phenomenon:

". . . Prostitutes who attempt to deceive (jive) their patrons, or unresponsive wives who similarly attempt to make their husbands believe that they are enjoying coitus, fall into an error because they assume that an erotically aroused person should look happy and pleased and should smile and become increasingly alert as he or she approaches the culmination of the act. On the contrary, an individual who is really responding is as incapable of looking happy as the individual who is being tortured."

Within seconds after sexual arousal the blood supply in the veins and arteries lying close to the skin increases, causing the body to become flushed and the temperature to rise slightly. Certain areas of the body are engorged with this blood, become swollen and erect, notably the penis of the man, which swells, often to twice its size. In women, this also happens to the clitoris, which becomes firm, and to the nipples of both sexes. The firmness of these organs increases, as the sexual climax approaches.

Muscles throughout the body begin to tense at the onset of sexual excitement, and this tension increases as the excitement grows. Certain glands and tissues also increase their secretions as the sexual act commences and moves closer to completion. The salivary glands and the nasal mucosa flow freely, and it is this latter fact which causes, in conjunction with the engorgement of the surface blood vessels, the characteristic nasal stuffiness so many people notice after intercourse. In some women the secretions of the glands of Bartholin and the mucus from the cervix of the uterus become amazingly copious as sexual excitement rises, and particularly during orgasm itself. This profuse flow may have given rise to the widely held and entirely mistaken idea I have mentioned—that in orgasm women have an ejaculation similar to the male's. There is no such ejaculation—nor indeed any female organ that could make one possible.

One of the most amazing aspects of sexual intercourse is the fact that all five senses become extremely dulled as the act increases in intensity. The ability to feel hot and cold, to feel pain, or to hear sounds becomes almost nonexistent. The eyes take on a charactehistic trance-like stare, and vision becomes constricted. The entire mind and body are concentrated fully on the mounting sexual feeling and exclude all else. In orgasm itself the anesthesia of the senses is almost total. Indeed many people experience a temporary loss of consciousness for a matter of seconds. Some, according to Kinsey's findings, remain unconscious for two or more minutes.

This last fact brings us to our examination of the experience of orgasm itself. If you are to understand frigidity in women it is of tremendous importance to grasp the nature of orgasm and what it means physically and psychologically. The importance of such understanding is due, of course, to the fact that orgasm, of the type described here, is the very thing the frigid woman is unable to have. In fact, its absence from her experience is the usual definition of frigidity. Certain kinds of frigid women may experience one, two, or all of the physical and psychological reactions described above, which normally would terminate with orgasm. But the final experience eludes them; at the vital juncture the body, despite an agonizing need to come to a climax, refuses to respond; it draws back, goes dead.

Orgasm is the physiological response which brings sexual intercourse to its natural and beautiful termination. It is preceded by a very dramatic increase in all of the phenomena noted above. In the moment just preceding orgasm, muscular tension suddenly rises to the point where, if the sexual instinct were not in operation, it would become physically unendurable. The pelvic motions of the man and the movement of the penis back and forth within the vagina increase in speed and in intensity of thrust. The woman's pelvic movements also increase, and her whole body attempts with every move to heighten the exquisite sensations she is experiencing within her vagina. According to many women with whom I have discussed this experience, the greatest pleasure is caused by the sensation of fullness within the vagina and the pressure and friction upon its posterior surface.

At the moment of greatest muscular tension all sensations seem to take one further rise upward. The woman tenses beyond the point where, it seems, it would be possible to maintain such tension for a moment longer. And indeed it is not possible, and now her whole body suddenly plunges into a series of muscular spasms. These spasms take place within the vagina itself, shaking the body with waves of pleasure. They are felt simultaneously throughout the body: in the torso, face, arms, and legs—down to the very soles of the feet.

These spasms, which shake the entire body and converge upon the vagina, represent and define true orgasm. At this moment the woman's head is thrown back and her pelvis tips upward in an attempt to obtain as much penetration from the penis as is possible. The spasms continue for several seconds in most women, though the time varies with every individual, and in some women they may continue though with decreasing intensity, for a minute or even more.

Many women can repeat this performance two or more times before their partner has his orgasm. The pathway, neurologically and psychologically, has been set for orgasm and, if her partner continues she can respond. I have had women report that the last orgasm is sometimes more intense and satisfying than the first.

If a woman is satisfied by her orgasmic experience she will discharge the neurological and muscular tension developed in the sexual build-up. When satisfaction has been achieved, her strenuous movements cease and within a short period blood pressure, pulse, glandular secretion, muscular tension, and all the other gross physical changes which characterize sexual excitement return to normal, or even to subnormal, limits.

There have been detailed studies made of the physical reactions of both men and women during intercourse. I think it is important to realize that in almost every detail, including orgasm, these reactions and the subjective experience of pleasure parallel each other in the sexes. The major differences are that the woman is slightly slower to respond at the outset than the man, and the orgasm of the man is characterized by the ejaculation of sperm into the vagina.

Full sexual satisfaction is followed by a state of utter calm. The body feels absolutely quiescent. Psychologically the person feels completely satisfied, at peace with the world and all things in it. The woman in particular feels extremely loving toward the partner who has given her so much joy, such a transport of ecstasy. Often she wishes to hold him close for a while, to linger tenderly in the now subdued glow of their passion.

As you can see from this description, orgasm is a tremendous experience. There is no physiological or psychological experience that parallels its sweeping intensity or its excruciating pleasure. It is unique.

There are many who take a mystical view of this ecstatic coupling of man and woman in love. They think of it as a symbol of a lost unity between the sexes that strives to reassert itself in the act of love. Others see in it a foretaste of heaven, the carnal representation of endless spiritual delights for mankind. Many who are able to experience orgasm in intercourse find it difficult not to ascribe some purposive intent on the part of the Creator; the experience is that profound.

The individual perceives orgasm as a reward equal to none. It puts the sacrifices and compromises necessary to an enduring marriage into their proper perspectives, makes the constant giving done by the woman seem not only worth while but highly desirable. It is the strongest link in the unbreakable bond between two who love.

Do you recall Tennessee Williams' play *A Streetcar Named Desire?* In one of its most famous passages the frigid (and promiscuous) older woman attempts to break up the marriage of her younger sister, appealing to a spurious pride of class, pointing out that the younger woman has married beneath her, married a beer-drinking, poker-playing common day laborer. The younger woman is almost convinced that she should act on the false values of her sister. After all, these values had been inculcated in both women by the same parents and they went deep. The young girl's husband saves her, however; he simply reminds her of the pinwheels she sees, of the high music of the bells she hears when they embrace in love. It is enough. She returns to him without a word. The bond of their wonderful sexual life is unbreakable, far stronger than the powerful and subtle assault the envious and destructive sister can make upon the marriage.

The ability to have a full orgasm is, in most cases, the hallmark of the psychologically mature woman. It is the sign that she has successfully weathered the storms of childhood and youth and come, unscathed, into full womanhood, with all that it implies.

Chapter 3

THE NOT IMPOSSIBLE SHE

What *is* the mature woman? Who is she? What are her characteristics? Her personality? Her role in life?

It is of vital importance to an understanding of the frigid woman to answer these questions, for again, only by understanding what health is, can we truly grasp the meaning of any departure from it.

There have been great arguments about what the word "normal" means. Millions of words have been written about it. I fear that most of them have only clouded the issue. Odd definitions of normalcy have led millions of women down very odd and unhappy paths. You will recall, for example, that Victorianism elevated frigidity to the position of the norm for all womankind—with disastrous results.

At the start of my practice I encountered another strange and tragic view of the normal that has had a powerful influence on American women. This view, which we will encounter in more detail when the feminist movement is discussed later, still has wide repercussions and is intimately bound with the subject of frigidity and divorce.

In my introduction to it a lovely woman of forty came to consult me. She was deeply disturbed and could hardly speak, she wept so. Somehow I felt at once that there was a deep rage behind those tears. I recognized her name when she was able to get it out; she was a successful lawyer whose name many would still recognize in all probability.

In her thirty-ninth year she had fallen in love for the

first time with a fine man, another successful lawyer. Her dormant sexuality and true femininity had been awakened completely in her since their marriage a year before, and they both now wanted children badly. However, a physical examination had indicated (as unhappily it so often seems to do for women who postpone their first pregnancy for too long), that she would have to have a hysterectomy, for she had developed a tumor in the wall of her uterus.

She felt cruelly deprived, and I saw her for several sessions. During these periods she told me of her background. Her father had died when she was an infant and her mother had been a militant leader of the movement for women's "rights." The whole emphasis in her early upbringing had been on achievement in the male world, and in the male sense of the word. She had been taught to be competitive with men, to look upon them as basically inimical to women. Women were portrayed as an exploited and badly put upon minority class. Marriage, childbearing, and love were traps that placed one in the hands of the enemy, man, whose chief desire was to enslave woman. Her mother had profoundly inculcated in her the belief that women were to work in the market place at all cost, to be aggressive, to take love (à la Russe) where they found it, and to be tied down by nothing, no one; no more, as her mother put it, than a man is.

Such a definition of the normal had, of course, made her fearful of a real or deep or enduring relationship with a man. For years she sedulously avoided men entirely. Gradually, though her grown-up experiences, she learned of other values, but by the time the right man came along it was too late to have children.

I was right that her tears had been tears of rage. They were directed at her mother's authoritarian but totally mistaken view of the feminine role in life and were, to my mind, justified. When she had sufficiently vented her righteous anger, but not until then, we were able to move on to more practical matters. Her marriage was a happy one, and finally she adopted two children. With some of her values revised she made a wonderful mother for them. I visited this family only recently, and it seems to be one of the happiest and healthiest, psychologically speaking, I have ever seen.

Most women who have been reared with such ideas of what is normal are not so fortunate, however. They cling to their defensive and self-destructive values to the end, which is often bitter.

And there are, still, passionately convinced and often eloquent purveyors of these ideas. After reading the brilliant
best seller, *The Second Sex,* by Simone de Beauvoir, the
French authoress, I was saddened to see such clarity and
brilliance in the service of such a mistaken cause. Her tacit
conclusions seem to be that woman's historic role of wife
and mother are degrading to our sex, have kept woman from
her true destiny. As she describes what that true destiny is,
however, her clarity departs, and the role and function of
this woman of the future become more than merely vague.
Their foggy contours remind me of the glamorous-sound-
ing but totally evanescent and mist-enshrouded goals that
many of the frigid and lonely women I treat have when
they first come for help.

There is *no* vagueness about the goals, functions, and
needs of the normal woman. Science in recent years has
thrown a bright light on her, and that is why we can be
certain of many fundamental details about her. She is a mature, fully functioning woman, a woman who has realized
the better part of her potentialities, who knows how to
achieve and handle love and happiness, who has won
through to a fully satisfying mental and sexual life.

I very frequently draw a word portrait of such a woman
for patients who come to consult me about their sexual
problem. It often makes them angry, and they deeply resent some of the characteristics of this idealized woman.
They call her all sorts of names: "a victim of the male,"
"an impossible ideal." One eloquent younger woman called
her "a faceless tramp," and I have heard older women,
brought up under a more inhibited code than exists now,
call her "a shameless hussy."

And yet despite the hostility that my portrait is often
greeted with there is soon other evidence in my troubled
listeners that they have been touched deeply by the idea
that such a picture of womanhood might conceivably be a
possibility for them. "Do you really think I could ever get
to be anything like that?" The yearning question, phrased
in any number of wistful ways, will inevitably come, despite the obvious hostility, the bristling defenses, the fact
that the speaker is scared blue of sex and motherhood and
all they mean.

You see, women want to find themselves, desperately
want to. And in this portrait they get a hint, often the first
they have ever had, of what to aim for, of the real potential
inside themselves.

I call this subject of my sketch 'idealized," and she is.

But I want to emphasize that she is not a personal idle day-dream of my own, based on airy nothingness; very much the contrary. Her characteristics are based on exact and thoroughly checked psychological and biological facts, facts upon which the leading scientists in this field are in general agreement. And she is a composite based on observations of women I have known, and not always clinically. If you stop to think as you read about her, you may realize that you have known such women too.

What, then, is she like? First of all to give us a frame for our portrait so that we can see what we *do* know more clearly, let me state what we cannot know about her; what, in fact, is irrelevant.

We don't know what she looks like. She may be tall or short, red-haired, blond, or brunette. She may have large breasts and round hips and sloping shoulders, or she may be small-breasted (or even flat-chested), have wide shoulders and narrow hips. She may have a career or not have a career, be more intelligent and better educated than her husband or less intelligent and less well educated. She may have children or be unable to have children. She may be rich or poor, come from the "400" or from the slums. She may be a bit shy or quite at ease socially. She may be athletic or totally unathletic. These things we don't know about her and, for our purposes, they do not matter.

Here are some of the things we do know.

In the first place, she is very much "at home" in the world. Deep inside herself she feels profoundly secure, safe, both with herself and with her husband. She is very, very glad to be a woman, with all the duties, responsibilities, and joys it entails. She can't imagine what it would be like to be a man and has no interest in imagining it as a possible role for herself. She feels that the very existence of her husband makes the world safe for her.

This feeling may seem unrealistic, in view of the very clear insecurities in the world today. As you will discover, however, it is based on a far deeper understanding of reality, on a far deeper reality than the one reflected in the alarums published in the daily newspaper.

This sense of reality almost invariably leads her to select a husband who is good for her, often near perfect, in fact. He might not be perfect for another woman, nor perfect in any ultimate sense, but he is near perfect for *her*. He loves her and intends to go on loving her. He may be a carpenter or an architect, a lawyer, a dock hand, or a poet, but he, with her, is passionate and loyal, a good com-

panion and a good father for her children. She has an in-
fallible sense about this matter, and though she may have
had an adolescent or college crush on a no-gooder, she simply never will marry him.

Of course marrying a good husband adds to her sense
of "at-homeness" in the world. Related to this feeling in her,
to her sense of security, seeming almost to spring from it,
indeed, is a profound delight in giving to those she loves.
Psychiatrists, who consider this characteristic the hallmark,
the *sine qua non*, of the truly feminine character, have a
name for it: they call it "essential feminine altruism."

As you will see, it too has its roots in woman's biology,
is, on its deepest level, a need in her that must have expression. The finest flower of this altruism blossoms in her joy
in giving *the very best of herself* to her husband and to her
children. She never resents this need in herself to give; she
never interprets its manifestations as a burden to her, an
imposition on her. It pervades her nature as the color green
pervades the countryside in the spring, and she is proud of
it and delights in it.

It is this altruism, this givingness, that motivates her to
keep her equilibrium, to hold onto her *joie de vivre* despite
whatever may befall. It stands her in marvelous stead for
all the demands that life is going to make on her—and
they will be considerable. When a woman does not have
this instinctually based altruism available to her, or when
she denies that it is a desirable trait, life's continuous small
misfortunes leave her in a glowering rage, helpless and be-
side herself with self-pity.

Another fact about her which you may be surprised to
learn is that she is deeply religious—though not officially
or even consciously. In fact, if her husband's background
has been antagonistic to formal religion and he is still reflecting his background, she may pay lip service to his ag-
nosticism or even atheism. But that doesn't mean a thing.
Just beneath the surface is an absolutely firm belief in the existence of a Creator and in some form of heaven. She's
not so clear about hell.

She also believes firmly in the fact that marriage is a
sacrament, binding forever. Given the slightest encouragement or support, she will formalize these beliefs, join a
church or develop a kind of personal pantheism. Why? Biologically speaking, she is the carrier of immortality, of the
generations of man. This gives her a close affinity to and
appreciation of the awesome and creative mysteries of the

universe: moonrise, tidal flow, the growth, death, and re-birth of things.

Sexually she almost always reaches a climax during the act of love. Sometimes she reaches two or, if she and her husband are feeling particularly lusty, even three. But the number of times is unimportant, despite the Kinsey report.

What *is* important is the *kind* of orgasm she has. It is of the kind described in the previous chapter, of course; the kind that starts deep within her vagina and extends to all parts of her body. She doesn't talk about it very often, but when she does it is always poetically. I have heard one woman refer to it as "a sensation of such beauty and intensity that I can hardly think of it without weeping"; of it another said, "It's like a mounting symphony, rising in tremendous and irresistible rhythms till your whole being feels as though it has been swept away." One woman, less lyrical but still exact, said, "It's like going over Niagara Falls in a barrel." Nobody can ever *quite* evoke the exact sensations in words, but, as one woman told me, "Nobody who has ever had it will doubt whether her experience is the real thing."

What else characterizes her sexually? Well, she's not very modest, I'm afraid. In fact, she's quite a show-off and likes sexual compliments from her husband, dressed or undressed, verbal or otherwise. Her nineteenth-century sister would have been vastly shocked by her whole attitude in the bedroom.

She's not sexually shy at all. She wouldn't demur a moment at initiating love with her husband, though she will immediately change her amorous direction if she finds he is too tired or is preoccupied, without feeling the least bit rejected. Don't forget that, for one thing, just under the surface (and sometimes on it) she considers her marriage a heaven-made arrangement that is going to last forever, and she need not look upon any one experience as too important in itself.

However, there is another very important point. I have indicated that sexually she takes her cue from her husband. What does she know, do you suppose—know deeply and instinctively—that makes her do this, while other women refuse to?

She knows this: that it is the man who, from the purely physical viewpoint, has to be ready before sexual intercourse can take place. No matter how many books have been written that ignore the fact, it is nevertheless true that, if the man does not have an erection, love-making cannot take place.

Just think about it for a moment. A woman *can* make love at any time; a man only when he is ready. There may be psychologically preferential circumstances for a woman, but there is no physical prerequisite.

That is why (by virtue of that deeper sense of reality we spoke of) when her husband is ready to make love our lady is nearly always willing, barring sickness or certain difficulties that may come up during pregnancy. And that is why she is always willing to forgo love-making if he is not ready. Her deep altruism makes her extremely sensitive to his moods, and she will not find it in herself to treat him as if he were a robot, become angry or feel rejected when, if the button is pushed, he doesn't respond.

On this same point: she knows how much store men put on their potency, how vulnerable they can become if they are made to feel inadequate to the needs of a wife. She would die a thousand deaths rather than have her husband gain any such inference from her actions. It's her altruism again.

Her eternal acquiescence, her ever-readiness, never lets her in for a painful sexual experience, however. She knows that ninety-nine times out of one hundred even negative sexual feelings in herself will soon return to eagerness, and eagerness to desire. And even if that once in a hundred times occur, she will still get a profound satisfaction from the pleasure she is able to give her husband, the very obvious pleasure. Once more that deep altruism.

But she not only takes the lead from him about *whether* they are going to make love—the *kind* of love they are going to make is also usually his decision and, in pure delight, she follows him completely. If he feels purely lusty, soon she does too; does he feel gentle and tender, then she picks up that mood. Experimental? Let's, by all means, experiment. Passive? She'll be active. It takes her little time to find out that a geisha has the tremendous disadvantage of believing that techniques are more important than love and the love of following one's partner.

Despite her very pronounced wantonness with her husband, however, she has no promiscuous urges whatsoever. She is realistic about other men and finds them attractive or unattractive, as the case may be. But she neither desires them nor has any fantasies of a sexual nature about them. One woman put it this way to me: "I like other men if they're attractive," she said. "Their attractiveness does honor to the sex my husband belongs to."

Nor is she ever tempted to indulge in self-masturbation, at least not after one or two tasteless and pointless experiments she may make during her first absence from her husband. To her, sexuality is devoid of any meaning whatsoever if there is not mutuality, if it is not shared

Lest you think that our paragon's altruism could end up by making her a martyr, a person without any real regard for herself, I must hasten to nip that idea in the bud. In her quiet way she is quite self-centered. In the first place, she's contented with all aspects of her body, all the details of a female anatomy that gives her so much pleasure. If in her cultural background there were influences which tended to inculcate disgust with certain natural functions, she finds herself rejecting them. For example, I have had several patients who, during the course of their therapy and as they found a new maturity developing in them, find themselves ruminating on the word "curse" as it is used to describe the menstrual flow. Reflection almost always makes them drop the word from their vocabulary entirely. In the end they are far more likely to call it a blessing.

This self-love, her pride in and love of her body, is reflected in her outward appearance. She likes to be as clean as a cat and as neat as a pin. She enjoys dressing well. She is very aware of the things that bring out her special attractiveness. She also knows how to make herself up to the very best advantage. But she does not spend hours daily on her toilet in front of the mirror. She is far too confident of herself, has too much self-love, to feel that such a production is necessary.

Here's the way I'd put it. She accepts and is pleased with the way she is and the way, as time passes, she is going to be. This is true of her mental capacities as well as of her physical attributes, but we can see it most clearly in her attitude toward her physical self. As I said at the beginning, we don't know whether she has small breasts or large breasts, rounded hips or narrow hips. We only know that, whatever she's got, she enjoys.

You see, she knows perfectly well that it is passion and response which spin the plot of love and not, ever, fetish or fashion. She really feels sorry for women who worry about what they haven't got or the effect of growing older. If she were small-breasted she would never disguise that fact, and you can be certain that her husband, at least after the relationship had got under way and he'd had a chance to experience her pleasures, would soon drop any adolescent predilections he had imagined he possessed.

The husband of one such woman said to me: "When I was in college I had a conviction that really beautiful women had to be redheads. I can't imagine now *what* made me believe such a thing." I know his wife well; she's a brunette, and you and I might not be the least bit impressed by her looks. But he knows better; he knows her real beauty. And, I happen to know, so does she.

The confidence and pleasure our fair lady has in her person and in her other attributes (her self-love) have one very odd quality. And it is an all-important one. This self-love is *detachable*.

With a flick of her psyche she can project practically all of it onto her children, take as much joy from their beauty, achievements, and pleasures as she ever got from her own. She detaches it, too, on behalf of her husband, often will exaggerate his good qualities and minimize any weakness he might have, as long as the weakness is not a danger to family and home.

Her detachable self-love and her need to give unrestrainedly are two chief components of the maternal instinct. To put it mildly, as perhaps you have noticed, she is pervaded with this instinct. To her the fulfillment of it is the most central and all-important function of her life. It colors and deepens and enriches her sexual life with her husband. Her unconscious fantasy with every intercourse is that he might make her with child, and her psychological and biological gratitude to him for this richest of all potential gifts is boundless. Her fantasies about becoming pregnant may excite her directly.

I have paid particular attention to this connection between the sexual instinct and the maternal instinct in many patients of mine who have come to therapy because they were afraid of childbirth. When they have been able to rid themselves of such fears they are almost always struck by the new dimension that is added to their sexual life. The things they say about it are often poetic or even mystical.

One woman, who because of childhood experiences had been scared to death of bearing a child and whose fear was causing a partial frigidity, said to me of her new sexual experience: "I was living in one room of a whole mansion, and now I have the whole mansion for my own." Another woman, who had believed her love life complete despite her deep fear of pregnancy, said of the change in her feelings during love-making: "Oh, it was fun before, but now the idea that I might become pregnant makes me feel at one with the whole universe. It's strange. There are almost no words to express it."

Our ideal woman carries this characteristic feeling of a deep identification with nature, with all things that grow and bud and blossom, through her pregnancy and long thereafter. Childbirth has no real terrors for her; she sails through it proudly, like a clipper made especially for such weather.

And she usually wants to nurse her child at her breast. She does, too, unless a breast abscess or some other unforeseen difficulty arises. And, though I have no statistics to prove it, I would bet that her milk is both plentiful and good.

I know that today there is a tremendous emphasis on the importance of careers for women, but I am afraid that our mature woman cannot get terribly excited about the subject. I don't mean that she's antagonistic to this whole modern movement. She may be a career woman herself, a nurse, a doctor, a lawyer, a fashion designer, whatever. But now, happily married and with children in the offing or already here, she can't feel that it's of central importance. If it's necessary for the family welfare she will keep her job, but any drive she had after high school or college to go far in it is sacrificed, if necessary, to her love-making and home-making instincts.

She is not the least bit jealous of her husband's work. As I pointed out earlier, she may be smarter than her husband or may basically have a much higher intelligence quotient, or she may be far more thoroughly educated than he is. Or she may be highly talented in some art form—writing, music, painting, sculpture. You will never, however, hear her complain that she gave up a career for her family, or angrily envy the daily adventures of her man in the market place. Her joy and satisfaction in the fulfillment of her own biological destiny make all other personal achievements pale for her, any other considerable use for her energies almost a waste.

As she grows older and her family grows up and the children learn to stand on their own feet and use their own wings, she may return to work. However, even then, interest in her now-grown children and their children will be far greater than any she can summon up for her job.

As you might expect, our paragon ages very gracefully.

Those sure instincts which led her to successful love in marriage and to success in rearing her children stand her in good stead now. She still loves to give, and she perceives the right time to give her children up, to let them stand on their own, learn the difficult uses of freedom. Admittedly this is a great sacrifice for a mother, but she is deeply pleased to make it. And in doing so without fuss or feathers, she wins her children's regard and love forever.

I am very pleased to say that the menopause brings no diminution in her ability to enjoy her husband sexually. Contrary to what many people still think, her orgasm does not decrease in intensity or in kind. Increasing age and the absence of children in the home now bring her and her husband closer together again and, great companions, they develop a whole series of shared pleasures consistent with their years.

As she goes down into the other side of her middle years, she is not troubled with regrets for things left undone. She has a deep sense of fulfillment, of life lived rightly. And, whether she has become consciously religious or not, she is still, basically, a believer in immortality, for she has served it with her whole being. She looks on death totally unafraid, wondering perhaps what the Creator who has made her life such a marvel is like on an even closer view.

This, then, is the idealized picture of the truly feminine woman. While granting that the plane of maturity she has achieved is rather too exalted for most women to attain, I have given her to you for some very concrete reasons.

With merely this ideal to follow, I have seen many women reap immediate rewards some time before they were able to come to grips with their frigidty per se. The characteristics and neurotic goals that accompany frigidity often cause obvious domestic frictions that can be greatly reduced when the woman begins to see new horizons for herself—that she need not be blaming others. Her grateful husband will reward her at once for her change, with renewed affection and tenderness, a new solicitude, a new caring.

Our idealized portrait can help you, too, to grasp more thoroughly the rest of this book. We have found, in psychiatry, that when a goal has been clearly defined half the battle has been won. As we come now to the chapters on frigidity, its history, its whys and wherefores, kinds and causes and cures, you will have before you a picture of what the potentialities of women are, a landmark to show you how far our sex can stray from real femininity, a guide to keep you from confusion, from ever subscribing again to false and destructive ideas of what it is that constitutes real womanhood.

Chapter 4

WHAT IS FRIGIDITY?

Now that we have seen the real potential of woman, how she can flower and blossom in the climate of love, what she can be like when she embraces her true destiny, we may turn to an examination of frigidity with some perspective. This section will deal with what frigidity is, specifically, and why it can and does occur in women, blighting their capacities, stunting their personality, chilling and killing their ability to love at the heart's deep core. When a woman gets a clear picture of such matters, and *only* when she does, can she find her way back to the highroad of real womanhood.

If we take the word "frigidity" in its most general sense it means, as I have already stated, an inability to enjoy sexual love to its fullest potentiality. This means, purely and simply, the inability to have an orgasm of the type described in Chapter 2. But the matter is more complicated than that, for there are degrees of frigidity, and I think it is very important to understand what this means.

Perhaps I can make this idea clearest by first describing the symptoms of a woman who came to see me several months ago. She was an example of total sexual frigidity.

In our first interview she described herself as having absolutely no sexual reactions whatsoever. She did not respond to her husband's caresses in any way at all. Neither her clitoris, vagina, nor labia was capable of the slightest sexual response. She received no stimulation from kissing or physical closeness. Her breasts and all secondary erotic regions were, from the standpoint of sensual response, dead. Her vaginal passage never became lubricated before or during intercourse. The act of love was very painful for her. An examination by a competent gynecologist showed no physical condition which would explain her pain. Her external genitalia were all fully developed. Her reproductive organs—the vaginal tract, cervix, uterus, tubes, and ovaries—also were normally developed and showed no pathology.

This woman's sexual unresponsiveness was entirely psychological, and on a scale showing the degree of frigidity she would represent absolute zero. (This is no longer true of her, incidentally; she has made progress in therapy in a relatively short time, considering the extent of her difficulty, and her final prognosis promises to be excellent.)

At the opposite end of this frigidity scale is the woman who trembles on the verge of sexual maturity but cannot quite step over the line. In the act of love she has all the responses which I have described as taking place in normal sexual intercourse, but she cannot come to orgasm, or at least orgasm happens quite rarely—say once in ten or twenty times—and it is generally a mild and unsatisfactory one. You will be interested to know that her sexual problem is a relatively easy one to resolve. This is the kind of frigidity that may disappear entirely after the birth of a child. I have seen it dispelled, too, by a single conversation with a wise counselor or with just time and a minimum of insightful understanding which she can obtain by taking thought or learning more about the nature of her problem and dispelling certain misunderstandings she has had about the nature of sex, marriage, men, and love.

In between these two types there are all degrees of sexual frigidity. The severity of a woman's problem, or the lack of it, can be calculated in terms of the degree of response she has to her husband's caresses and the frequency with which she achieves satisfaction in intercourse. Also important in estimating the degree of the problem is the orgasm itself. This is purely a subjective matter and can of course be judged only by the individual. If the orgasm is weak and chronically leaves one with a dissatisfied feeling, a certain degree of frigidity is present.

In addition to the *degrees* of frigidity there is a *type* of frigidity that it is very important to understand. We call a woman suffering from this form of frigidity a "clitoridal" or "masculine" type. To make her problem clear to you I shall have to describe her typical sexual reaction.

This woman's responses to sexual stimulation are usually quite passionate. In the foreplay preceding sexual intercourse and even in the first part of intercourse her reactions parallel the normal to a greater or lesser extent. This type of woman, however, can always be identified by the kind of orgasm she has.

This orgasm takes place on her clitoris exclusively. She does not feel the orgasm in her vagina, nor do the sexual sensations spread very strongly to the other parts of her body. The sensual experience is primarily localized at climax, and though, owing to her lack of experience with the mature form of orgasm, she may defend her orgasm as perfectly normal and adequate, it is not. Therapy has helped many women with this constricted reaction to sexual intercourse and, once they have experienced the profound pleasure of the true orgasm, they will admit quite freely their former deprivation.

The clitoridal woman seeks to obtain her typical orgasm in two ways. In intercourse she will sometimes strive to bring her clitoris into direct contact with the penis, thus obtaining the stimulation necessary for her to achieve climax. Most women, however, are not able to gratify themselves in this way. Intercourse seems to deaden their sexual feelings, even their clitoral feelings. It is as though the male penis in the vagina represented a dangerous and hostile presence. Such women are only able to come to their clitoridal climax either by masturbating themselves or having their husbands do so before or after intercourse.

The clitoridal woman—that is, the woman who experiences orgasm on her clitoris alone—is very definitely suffering from a form of frigidity. Indeed this form of frigidity is extremely widespread, and we will devote much space to it later, tracing the origin of the difficulty and the indications for treatment.

Since we have a name for the clitoridal type of sexual frigidity, let us, for the sake of clarity, also give a name to the form of frigidity first described, that which is characterized by a subnormal degree of sensation in the entire genital area and weak and infrequent orgasm. This form of frigidity is called sexual anesthesia in textbooks, and I will use that phrase here when I refer to it. The word "anesthesia," as you probably know, simply means the absence, or relative absence, of sensation.

Now that we have named names I should like to say that I wish the problem of frigidity were as uncomplicated as this description makes it sound. If it were we'd simply have the problem of a large number of women who weren't getting all the pleasure out of life that is possible. But there is far more to it than that.

The sad fact is that frigidity usually has a profound psychological repercussion on the individual. Her inadequacy is rooted in her childhood or adolescence, in early fears and misunderstandings, in events largely forgotten now. Around these early experiences, as crystals around a string, have clustered a whole series of personality traits that make life very hard for her and, much too often, unbearable for those nearest and dearest to her—her husband and her children.

To put it most directly, frigidity is generally a product of neurosis. And, most importantly, the frigid woman's neurotic behavior is in direct proportion to the degree of her frigidity. I have found it to be true that, the more frigid a woman is, the more neurotic her behavior becomes, the more inimical to her own good and to the good of her family.

It is these psychological repercussions that make the problem of frigidity a serious one for the individual and society. The frigid woman's often grossly neurotic psychological traits are raising havoc with our marital institution in the form of unhappiness, divorce, and maladjustment in her children.

Women will usually face the fact that they are sexually frigid; generally they have to; the knowledge is forced upon them. But they will rarely face the fact that they have personality difficulties that are directly related to their obvious sexual difficulty.

Let me give you an illustration.

Last year a very intelligent woman came to see me. She was an associate professor of history at a leading university and, according to her, her only complaint was that she could not have an orgasm during intercourse. She was unusually frank in describing the sexual aspect of her problem in her first interview, and when she had finished the description of her reactions and lack of them she had described a woman with a rather severe sexual anesthesia. She had neither clitoral nor vaginal sensation and could claim only some vaguely pleasant sensations on her labia. She had nothing approximating an orgasm.

Actually she was a very fine woman, but she was totally confused about this area of her life. "If I could only break through this silly little block," she told me, "our marriage would be ideal." I could get no further real facts from her. She insisted that she and her husband had "a whole community of shared interests" and two "wonderfully normal" children. I asked to see her husband.

I got the real story from him. He was, he told me, quite worried about his wife and about their marriage and had been for a long time.

She had always, he said, been an extremely competitive woman, but since his promotion from associate professor to full professor four years before, this characteristic had become almost unendurable. "I hardly dare to open my mouth any more," he told me, "because I know she's going to contradict me." Quarrels had become extremely frequent, and their oldest child was definitely showing neurotic signs. I inquired about her reactions during her pregnancies, and he told me that she had been constantly ill physically and, while she would not admit it, had clearly been deeply frightened of the whole experience. Indeed, after the birth of the second child she had become severely depressed for over two months. He told me that yes, indeed, they had *had* a community of interests for the first couple of years of their marriage but that her competitiveness with him had become so pronounced that any mutuality, from his standpoint, was now almost impossible.

Any psychiatrist knowledgeable in such matters could have guessed from the woman's description of her sexual problem pretty much what I learned about her from her husband. For, as I have pointed out, the kind and degree of frigidity a woman may confess to are also an open statement of the kind and degree of personality distortion she is subject to.

As one might guess, this patient was not easy to treat. She had developed a powerful tendency to handle her fears by denying their existence. When she was finally able to see through this self-deceiving trait, however, she came to grips with her problem. She was able to see that she had been in a ten-year competition with her husband instead of a marriage. When she realized this she was able to control her competitive actions, and the immediate rewards she received in the form of renewed affection and companionship from her grateful husband motivated her to find out more and more about herself. At length this intelligent but dreadfully insecure person became, through understanding and insight, a real woman able to give and take in every aspect of the love relationship.

Frigidity causes a personality distortion. I wish to impress this on you deeply. It means that the person has a misunderstanding of reality, denies it, blames others for her own miseries and failures.

One woman who had been cured of a severe frigidity problem phrased it this way: "I was looking at life and people through a distorting glass. No wonder I made such poor decisions." She was right, too. Her problem had first driven her to promiscuity, then to marriage with an alcoholic. I was very glad, when she first came for treatment, that she had not yet had any children. With her deeply seated, sexually based personality problem she might have ruined them. I am even gladder that, remarried to a fine man, she has two children now.

In a later section we shall examine in great detail these personailty problems that accompany frigidity. There are, however, more immediate symptoms which I should like to go into here.

You will recall in the description of sexual intercourse leading to orgasm how thoroughly the body becomes mobilized: heartbeat, pulse, and blood pressure rise precipitately, tissues become engorged with blood, glands secrete freely, muscular tension mounts to a pitch which would be unendurable if the sexual instinct were not demanding expression. Complete satisfaction brings an end to all these processes, and the energy discharged through normal channels and in a normal manner leaves the person in a condition of relaxation and with a sense of well-being.

When orgasm does *not* take place, when there is no release of the intensely mobilized energy, there are immediate repercussions, both physical and psychological, on the individual.

Psychologically the woman who has been brought to such a pitch experiences a feeling of acute frustration which, consciously or unconsciously, turns to anger at herself and at her partner. If the anger is unconscious, she may have physiological symptoms—headache, nausea, throat constrictions, heart palpitations, or difficulty with breathing. She may also weep uncontrollably, vomit, or have tremors throughout her body.

This unconscious anger at her frustration may also cause her to quarrel with her husband or to take out her rage on the children.

I should like to emphasize that she usually does not see any connection between these symptoms and her frustrated sexual experiences. When her anger at her frustration does become conscious, she usually blames her husband for her lack of satisfaction. As I have pointed out, he is rarely to blame.

Purely physical symptoms not connected with repressed anger may also follow upon sexual excitement which has not been released through orgasm. These are somatic and can probably be traced to undischarged neuromuscular and glandular energy. Such symptoms include low back pain, general restlessness, and very often acute insomnia. Several of my patients have complained of severe vaginal pains which have lasted several hours. Gynecologists report that abdominal cramps, probably emanating from contractions of the uterus, are frequent.

As you can see from this recital of symptoms and my preliminary descriptions of personality disorder, women may pay a very high price for their frigidity. If the condition were relatively rare, we could take some comfort from *that* fact at least.

But frigidity is not rare; it is one of the commonest and most serious chronic ailments that beset society today. Conervative estimates indicate that 40 per cent of all American women suffer from some degree or kind of sexual frigidity. No other public health or social problem of our time even approaches this magnitude.

I have now told you about the degrees and psychological consequences of frigidity and described one basic type. There are, however, two other types of frigidity which, because they have certain confusing elements in them, I have reserved until now to explain. Psychologically and sexually both of these types seem to run counter to the generalities I have made about frigidity so far.

The first type, though we consider her definitely frigid in the wide sense of the word, is able to have full and complete orgasm practically every time she has intercourse. This is really quite an astonishing fact, considering the usual close connection between personality and sexuality. Actually one could not distinguish in any way the sexual reaction of this type from that of the perfectly normal woman described in Chapter 3.

However, this kind of woman is totally unable to build a relationship with any man. For that reason she generally becomes, in the end, sexually promiscuous. Somehow and somewhere along the line a wedge has been driven between her sexuality and her ability to relate psychologically in a love relationship. Her sexuality has come to apparent maturity while her character has remained infantile. We call this psychic frigidity.

This type of woman is not, however, to be confused with the nymphomanic woman, who, in my experience, is generally seriously mentally disturbed and for that reason is not included in this book. The woman with psychic frigidity usually has sexual affairs with one man at a time; her neurosis is usually based on sexual seduction in early childhood.

The second type is nearly the exact opposite of the psychic type of frigidity. I call her the all-mother type. She is a distinct anomaly. In the first place, she is definitely classifiable as sexually frigid; the degree of her erotic reaction is zero. She is totally anesthetic sexually.

Psychologically speaking, however, she exhibits almost the perfect picture of normalcy. She is happily married, is a very giving and altruistic person, and is totally loyal and devoted to her husband. She is, above all, a wonderful mother, willing and able to give the very best of herself to her children. Her husband is generally happy with his marriage. We suspect, although there is not sufficient data on this to say it with certainty, that the mate of the all-mother type has a rather low-pitched sexual nature and also a rather low storehouse of normal male vanity, albeit he is a good provider and a steady type. It is probable that the woman divined his characteristics unconsciously when she first fell in love with him.

There is generally little reason why the all-mother type of woman should seek to change herself in any way. I must emphasize the fact again and again that the reason frigidity presents a problem that must be solved is that it has harmful repercussions on the woman and on those close to her. It causes acute misery to her, causes personality damage to the children, and tends to destroy her marriage. The all-mother type of frigidity does none of these things, and I see no reason, if the woman doesn't, why she must contemplate changing herself. However, the matter can be a subtle one, for this type of woman can, without any awareness of the fact, tend to be overprotective of her children or tend to have a hard time letting them go from the nest when that period in their growth has arrived. She should be most careful, weigh this matter thoroughly, before she decides in any final sense whether her problem may or may not be having untoward effects of a concealed nature.

These, then, are some of the basic facts about the nature of frigidity. Let us now consider their implications.

Chapter 5

THE WAR BETWEEN MEN AND WOMEN

When one contrasts the normal woman with the frigid woman, certain questions come to mind at once. Why, for exmple, *do* certain women become frigid? Have millions of women always been this way, or is it a problem of our times only? Why, if *not* being frigid is so pleasant, do some women hold onto this problem though they know they can get help for it?

To answer these questions in part or in whole, you will first have to know a little history. For, though every case of frigidity represents a psychological problem in the individual, we have found that, sociologically speaking, frigidity is rooted in certain destructive events that have occurred to woman in the past two hundred years. If you grasp them you will begin to get a picture of the over-all problem that has beset woman, of how she lost her direction, her sense of self, and what she must do to find them again.

The history I am going to tell you about is the history of a war, a bitter and destructive war. It is often called "The War between Men and Women." For far too many women and men too—it is still going on.

It began toward the end of the eighteenth century, and the apparently innocent event that started it all was the invention of the steam engine by Watt—the great invention that ushered in the modern age. It seems hard to believe now that this almost outdated means of creating power could have been so important, but it was. It launched the so-called Industrial Revolution, which was to change the whole fabric of society, our ways of doing things and making things, our living quarters and our living standards, our morals, religion, art; name it and you will find that the Industrial Revolution has turned it upside down and inside out.

Most of all, and most tragically, it changed the home. It would be more accurate, if somewhat bleaker, to say that it destroyed the home, at least as home was known up to that time.

But let me tell you what home was like before the Industrial Revolution, for when you see that you will begin to discern the outlines of the great tragedy that happened to woman when the old-fashioned family home ceased to exist.

In that era our society was almost entirely rural and agricultural. In other words, most homes were farms. There were cities and some industry, of course, but where industries existed they were almost entirely home industries run by individual families.

Home, then, was, almost without exception, the center of all life, economic, social, and educational. Everything was produced at home; all food was grown; suits and dresses and underclothing were made from cloth woven on the premises. There were simply no stores in which to buy anything. The leather for shoes was taken from the hides of animals one had reared oneself, and the shoes were made at home, the leather tanned, the shoes fashioned. A man made his own tools, was his own blacksmith, carpenter, architect. He built his own house, too, and kept it in repair.

Woman's place in this early family home was indisputably at the very center, an equal partner with her husband in all the manifold duties, responsibilities, joys, hopes, and fears of the entire household. Her work was heavy and constant; she cooked the food her husband had grown, wove the cloth, fashioned and made the clothes for the entire family. She cleaned and she swept, washed, and ironed from morning till night.

Children, as soon as they were old enough, lightened her labors. She was responsible for their education (public schools had never been heard of), which was not just a matter of teaching them the three R's but of inculcating in them all that she knew of the multitude of arts, crafts, and techniques it took to run such a home.

Her reward for all this was the fact that she was needed,

loved, held in the highest esteem by her husband and her whole family. If she failed in her duties or if she died, it would be not merely a sad or inconvenient event for the family. It would be a disaster, for the activities of the distaff side, although different from those of the male, were of equal importance.

There were of course no social scientists to ask her probing questions about her sex life, and we can only know about her indirectly and by piecing odd patches of information together wherever we may find them. From what we can gather, even the concept of frigidity in marriage was unknown to her; love, home, work were a unified and profoundly satisfying experience on all levels. As a woman she was profoundly needed, and as a woman reared to respond to this need she had no single occasion to question her worth or her abilities.

And then one by one, slowly but surely, her responsibilities and her duties were removed from her; her close and equal working relationship with her husband was destroyed; her importance to her children was diminished sadly.

The new machines made possible by Watt's harnessing of steam power began to take over, to displace all those things that had been done by hand. Transportation, via the new Iron Horse, developed, and trade between sections that were once remote from one another was made possible. A man could make more money than he had ever dreamed of if he could supply a need of some group or community.

And so industry in the sense that we know it today started with a rush. The principle of steam power was applied to the manufacture of goods with tremendous success. Factories sprang up, and they needed men to run them. Now husbands who but recently had worked at home, hand in hand and side by side with their wives, labored outside the home, developed lives that were independent to some extent of the home's activities and concerns.

The supply of manufactured goods from the factories began to render the homemaking skills and handicrafts of woman unnecessary. As time wore on and new ideas developed to meet the new conditions created by the machine, the education of the children passed from the home to a new institution, the public school.

It happened slowly, very slowly, over generations, in fact, and the full results of the Industrial Revolution were not felt until this century. At first, so gradual was the process that only a few women, scattered here and there, felt the impact of the change. But as time passed and the process extended, more and more families were drawn into the vortex of industrialization, and at length it had changed the lives of every individual in the land.

Very slowly, too, but everywhere, women woke as if from a centuries-old dream of peace and happiness to find themselves dispossessed. Gone was their central place in the family home, gone their economic importance, gone their close working partnership with their mate, their functions of teacher and moral guide to the children. The child himself was gone, to school, as the husband had gone to the mill or factory.

Yes, she was dispossessed, dispossessed of all those things that for centuries had defined her womanhood for her, that had supported her ego, given her the certain knowledge that being a woman, however hard, was a wonderous and most desirable thing. She felt her womanhood itself devalued, the things it represented unwanted.

And then she reacted. She reacted violently and with rage at this depreciation of her feminine attributes, of her skills, of her functions. Unhappily this reaction was precisely the wrong one, the one from which no solution of a happy kind for her could be attained.

Here's what she did. Looking about, she thought she spied a villain in the piece. Who was it? None other than her partner through the centuries, man. It was he who had deserted her, who was responsible for her loss of self-respect as a woman, a mother, an equal socially and mentally and morally. He despised women. Very well, she would show him. She would simply stop being a woman. She would enter the lists and compete with him on his own level. To hell with being a women. She would be a man.

You don't believe it? It seems too farfetched? Woman as a sex would never have made such a decision?

Well, let's look a little more closely at some of the facts.

Earlier I mentioned the feminist movement. Now it is time to look at it in more detail. It was launched by Mary Wollstonecraft in 1792, less than thirty years after the invention of the steam engine that ushered in the Industrial Revolution, and it's power and influence were and still are enormous. It has been the self-appointed spokesman for womankind for over one hundred fifty years, and its program of reforms has been almost entirely realized in every detail.

What did this movement want to achieve? Let me quote to you what two profound students of feminism, Ferdinand Lundberg and Marynia F. Farnham, had to say about it in their book *Modern Women, The Lost Sex*: "Far from being a movement," they wrote, "for the greater self-realization of women, as it professed to be, feminism was the very negation of femaleness. Although hostile to men and hostile to children, it was at bottom most hostile to women. It bade women commit suicide as women and attempt to live as men . . . Psychologically, feminism had a single objective: the achievement of maleness by the female, or the nearest possible approach to it. In so far as it was attained, it spelled only vast individual suffering for men as well as women, and much public disorder."

What was the program of the feminists? Actually Mary Wollstonecraft had enunciated it in its entirety in her book, *A Vindication of the Rights of Women*, and the movement never deviated from her original demands. She had stated that men and women were, in all fundamental characteristics, identical, and that therefore women should receive the same education as men, be governed by the same moral standards, do the same work, and have identical political rights and duties. Women were to be treated exactly as men in every detail of living, and the same demands were to be made on them.

The appeal of this program was enormous. Nineteenth-century woman felt: "Ah, if we could only achieve *this*, then we would be happy once again." The fact—and it's a dreadfully simple one—is that now, indeed, the entire program has been realized and modern woman, having reaped the benefits of it in full, is more confused, perhaps even unhappier, than ever.

Please do not misunderstand me. I am not saying that woman's lot was not difficult, often impossible, in the nineteenth century. Nor am I saying that all of the goals set by the feminists were neurotic and wrong-headed. The movement indeed helped to overcome some of the gravest dislocations in social and economic life caused by the upheavals that followed in the wake of the Industrial Revolution.

I *am* saying this: that in so far as the feminist movement pitted itself against the male, and at the same time advised woman to masculinize herself or divest herself of her feminine nature, it was dreadfully neurotic, and we have been reaping the whirlwind this movement started ever since.

The rage of the feminist was directed against herself. We know, for example, that to fulfill herself biologically —that is, to give birth to children—a woman must have security, the protection of the male, a permanent abode. Marriage has been society's answer to this feminine need from time immemorial. But the feminists pitted themselves against the institution of marriage. Woman, they held, had the right, even as men did, to be promiscuous sexually, to live with whom she pleased, for as long or as short a time as she pleased. If she wished to get married she should be able to do so, but she should also have the privilege of terminating this marriage when she wished to, when she tired of it.

We know, too, that maternal love for children, particularly love of her own children, is one of the major traits of womankind, as typical of her as her female anatomy. We know that only the very sickest women, mentally, will desert or neglect their children. Maternality is so deeply rooted in the biology of the female sex that its fierce protectiveness can be observed in many animals.

Maternality is a trap, said the feminists in effect, a bill of goods sold to women by men in order to keep them enslaved. Children should not be allowed in any way to interfere with the new freedom of women. Work, advised the feminists, right up to the last day of pregnancy. Then, mothers, get back to work as soon as possible. Put your child in the hands of some trained child handler or handlers. Public nurseries were advocated, pre-kindergarten groups were advocated; anything that "freed" the mother was advocated.

Freed the mother for what? you may well ask. To work in offices and factories as the men did, of course. To substitute boss for husband, to share the "privilege" of being hired or fired; to be, in short, men.

If space allowed I could continue with a long and circumstantial list of masculine goals which the feminists advocated. And I could give an equally long list of goals which ignored or denied the existence of feminine characteristics in womankind. Very few of the early feminists actually lived in the manner they prescribed. But it was as clear as crystal that they ardently desired to.

But here is the important thing to remember: The feminist credo thoroughly discredited truly feminine needs and characteristics and substituted male goals for female goals. There weren't so many feminists in actual numbers, but those there were, were incredibly vocal, and in the end their ideals and beliefs became the ideals and beliefs of millions of women.

But the feminist front was not the only front in this war between men and women; it was only the loudest and most militant. Unnoted, hidden, unknown even to the women themselves, the war against feminine sexuality, against the flowering of true womanhood, was being waged in every home in the land. The chaste and prim-lipped heroine of this front was Victorian woman, whom we already have had a look at. Let's take another quick one.

Her reaction to the loss of her position in the highly creative family home which had preceded the Industrial Revolution was just as violent as that of the feminist. But it was thoroughly unconscious. She had been rejected, her place taken from her, her sexual and maternal functions devalued. Very well. She had a perfectly good technique for dealing with the situation.

She simply denied the very existence of female sexuality. Sex, according to her, was exclusively a male characteristic; woman had none of it in her nature. Although this was a form of psychological revenge on the "rejecting" male, she was amazingly successful in convincing men in general, even the scientists of the day, that frigidity was indeed a basic attribute of the female.

Victorian woman was, of course, unconscious of her motives in affirming that she was biologically frigid. She entirely believed it herself, and there is much evidence to indicate that the individual woman was generally deeply shocked if she discovered she was not as unresponsive as she had been taught she was or wished to be. She kept any such reactions a very dark secret indeed.

Frigidity as an article of female faith died with the Victorian woman—a happy and mercifully early death during World War I. But the influence of Victorianism is still very much with us in our unconscious attitude toward sex and love.

This, then, is the heritage of woman today: On the one hand, from Victorian woman, a profound belief that she is and should be non-sexual, frigid, by natural law. On the other hand, from the feminists, that man is woman's natural enemy, that she should drop her femininity altogether, oppose man, supersede him, become him.

Please stop for a moment now to think what effect either of these two attitudes must have had on the marital life of a woman who held one of them. Her hostility to her husband and all the misery such hatred implies, we take for granted. But it was the effect on the children that was decisive.

I have treated, as I have told you, several women who had been raised by Victorian or feminist mothers. The attitudes inculcated into these patients in their childhood would make one's hair stand on end. Or it should. This is what they learned at their mother's knee: Shame about their bodies; shame about menstruation, and disgust with it, hatred of it, for it is a hallmark of womanhood; fear of pregnancy and childbirth; punishment for early and natural sexual feelings and experimentation; destruction and depreciation of the father as an ideal image for the child to love or to emulate. In general, women learned early and well to loathe their womanhood in all of its important manifestations.

Can you begin to see why most psychiatrists passionately agree with Dr. Marynia Farnham when she writes: "The most precise expression of unhappiness is neurosis. The bases for most of this unhappiness ... are laid in the childhood home. The principal instrument of their creation are women."

You may perhaps have noticed that I have coupled our feminist with our Victorian woman, and you may object that they really shouldn't be spoken of in the same breath. The feminists were, after all, for more and more sexual freedom; Victorian woman was anti-sexual. I feel that that is only superficially true. They were both, in their unconscious lives, against feminine sexuality. It is not possible for woman to be masculine sexually; to advocate that for her is exactly equal to demanding that she be frigid.

Of course feminism, as a conscious attitude toward sexuality, ultimately triumphed over Victorianism. Sexual freedom and all the other equal rights with men demanded for women by the feminists after World War I became the order of the day.

The flapper of the 1920's represented the unintended flower of the feminist philosophy of life, its definition of what constituted womanhood. As we know, the flapper was a caricature of woman, a cheap and shoddy imitation of the opposite sex, a second-class man. Happily, she did not survive as a conscious national ideal, but the philosophy that created her *did* survive. The depreciation of the goals of femininity, biological and psychological, became part and parcel of the education of millions of American girls. Homemaking, childbearing and rearing, cooking, the virtues of patience, lovingness, givingness in marriage have been systematically devalued. The life of male achievement has been substituted for the life of female achievement.

The feminist-Victorian antagonism toward men has survived too. It has been handed down from mother to daughter in an unbroken line for so many years now that, to millions of women, hostility toward the opposite sex seems almost a natural law. Though many a modern woman may pay lip service to the ideal of a passionate and productive marriage to a man, underneath she deeply resents her role, conceives of the male as fundamentally hostile to her, as an exploiter of her. She wishes in her deepest heart, and often without the slightest awareness of the fact, to supplant him, to exchange roles with him. She learned this attitude at her mother's knee or imbibed it with her formula. Little that she learns elsewhere counteracts it with any great effectiveness.

Clearly, then, if this is the historical direction women have taken, the individual woman who wishes to become a real woman must change this direction. This she can do only by taking thought, long thought. For among the women around her she will not necessarily find too much support for her wish to be entirely feminine.

For one hundred fifty years now women have blamed their problems on the outside world. They have used the very real difficulties created by revolutionary social changes to avoid the task of looking within for the real problem and the real solution. They have indulged in an orgy of finger-pointing and self-pity.

If the results had been different, if this attitude had brought them happiness and fulfillment, if feminism and Victorianism had made them good mothers and joyful wives, or even pleased them with their new place in industry, the game might have been worth the candle. But it hasn't been. The game has brought frigidity and restlessness and a soaring divorce rate, neurosis, homosexuality, juvenile delinquency—all that results when the woman in *any* society deserts her true function.

Last year a woman came to see me at the request of a lawyer she had consulted. She was on the verge of divorce, she told me. And then, her face distorted with rage, she said of her husband: "He will have to come crawling to me on his hands and knees before I will even think of forgiving him."

I questioned her and soon elicited the fact that she had been totally frigid from the first time she had had intercourse with her husband. Yet consciously she felt blameless in the difficulties that had arisen, self-righteous, indignant that her husband should find her anything but eminently desirable after five years of joyless love-making. With such an attitude, of course, she could never have made the slightest headway against her underlying problem, so, as I sometimes do, I told her in detail the history I have told you in this chapter. She listened, at first with hostility and then with the growing shock of self-recognition. Just by listening she developed a genuine concern for the very first time about her whole attitude. She left that session with an avowed intent to look more deeply and more thoroughly into the whole matter and to reshape her values. There was no more talk of divorce from her; just hard work on her real problem, and success, finally, in dislodging the cause of it.

Seeing one's own responsibility in a situation is often difficult. However, in this problem of frigidity, not to take the blame is even more difficult. It means—and has meant for millions—that one almost literally commits sexual suicide, embraces emotional isolationism as the proper condition for womankind.

Chapter 6

WHY WOMEN CAN BECOME FRIGID

Some time ago a young husband sat in my office. His
wife had come to me for help for a frigidity problem, and
after the first session he had asked her if he might see me. I
take that to be a good omen for a relationship, generally,
and I was not disappointed when I met him. He told me
very quickly that he did not care how long it might take for
his wife to get over her difficulty. "I'd stay with her even if
she didn't," he said in a low voice. "I don't love her problem, but I love her and I want you to know that I didn't
marry her for better only but for worse as well."

No matter how much a psychiatrist hears about love, its
difficulties and its triumphs, a statement like that always
moves one, makes one feel that tasks and difficulties have
been somehow lightened. In short, I liked him, and this
moved me to ask him about himself. "That's what I came
to tell you about," he said. "There's something I thought
just may be of some help."

What he wanted to tell me was the amazing similarity
between his background and his wife's, and as he talked on
I could see some of the reasons for his broad sympathy
with her problem. They were both children of farm people
and had been reared in the strictest of Puritan disciplines.
They were both the oldest children, and each had had two
brothers and a sister. Their mothers had hated and feared sexuality and had communicated quite freely to the children
their feeling that it was dirty and wicked. The fathers had

been punitive on the one hand and withdrawn on the other. This young man had broken away from home as early as possible and so had his wife. They had come to the city, gotten jobs in the same business, and here they had met.

I will take leave of our young husband now because the above facts illustrate the question I want you to ask yourself. However, in case some of my warmth toward him has come over to you, I can tell you that his marriage had a most happy outcome. His wife, motivated strongly, I am sure, by the sense of security his love gave her, was able to resolve her frigidity and the other neurotic problems which invariably accompany it.

But to the question: With almost identical backgrounds, why had the wife developed a rather severe frigidity problem and the husband remained perfectly normal sexually?

If you wish to extend that question you may ask yourself: Why is frigidity so widespread among women and sexual impotency so rare among men? We saw that under the adverse conditions caused by the Industrial Revolution women could, by the millions, abandon sexual gratification, convince the world and themselves that, biologically speaking, they were asexual beings. There was never the faintest suspicion that man, on the other hand, would or could abandon his sexual nature, no matter how difficult the going became. Men might develop neuroses, they might even take odd sexual directions, develop perversions, if their parents were sufficiently neurotic. But abandon sexual gratification en masse, they could not.

I think we now understand the answer to this problem, and I think it will be helpful for you to learn what we know about it. You will be able to see why the problem of frigidity is so basically *psychological* in nature, for one thing, and therefore why, when a woman's chief complaint is frigidity, we feel that if she really means business she can get over it.

There are three major reasons why frigidity can develop in women. I am going to treat two of them here and reserve one of them for the next chapter.

The Sexual Drive in Women

A lovely actress I was treating for a rather severe frigidity problem came for her regular hour one day and paused on the threshold of my office. She appeared different—her face was softer, her motions slower—she was elated, and I felt at once that she had experienced the first reward for the hard work she had put upon her problem.

I was right and shall never forget her method of telling it. She had on a lovely pink cape; its flowing lines and delicate color seemed to express the very essence of the feminine. As she stood smiling at me she unbuttoned the cape and with a beautiful gesture threw it on the floor between us. "Thus we can cast it away," she said. Then, stooping, she picked it up. "And *thus,*" she said, "we can put it on again," and with a flourish she put it back on her shoulders. That hour was a celebration of her new-found capacity.

Her histrionic gesture, expressive of so much happiness in her, was not only graceful but was deeply symbolic of woman's sexual nature. To see why this is so, let us first turn our attention to the biological meaning of the sexual drive.

You perhaps know that every animal is motivated by a profound instinctual need to preserve his species. His nature has developed those characteristics that ensure the ongoingness of his kind, lemmings excepted, perhaps. We know that characteristics that *do* ensure the species are, so to speak, more deeply rooted in the biology of a given animal than characteristics that are not absolutely necessary to the preservation of a species.

Now, in the human animal and in many other species, sexual intercourse is the basic method by which the species is continued. In this elemental instinctual activity the male deposits his sperm in the respective female, who then, within her body, nurtures and protects it until it is ready for birth.

But here's the important point: In order to deposit his sperm, the male *must have an orgasm.* If he did not, the sperm could not be deposited inside the female. Thus the male orgasm is absolutely necessary to the continuation of the species. If the male had ever lost his ability to have an orgasm the species would have disappeared from the face of the earth.

However, it is not a biological *necessity* for woman to have an orgasm to fulfill her sexual role. It is only necessary for her to receive the sperm. The mere reception of it, no matter how unresponsive she may be to the ardors of the male, fully discharges her duty to the species of mankind. Maternity, not orgasm, is her biological duty. She can be as frigid as the polar cap and it will not necessarily affect her ability to have children in the slightest degree.

Can you see the implications? One of my colleagues summed up the difference in this way: "To express it in a purely biological sense, the male orgasm is a necessity. The female orgasm is a luxury." This "necessary" aspect of the male orgasm explains why men, no matter how deeply disturbing their childhood experiences may be, rarely lose their ability to have an orgasm and why women so frequently do.

Please do not misunderstand me, however. I am *not* saying that the orgasm a woman has, when she is able to achieve it, is any less intense than a man's. Nor am I saying that it is not necessary to her psychological well-being, to her maturity, to be able to achieve it.

I *am* saying that a woman's ability to have an orgasm is far more subject to outside influences than a man's ability. It is in many ways more subject to the psychological experiences, the mental and moral traumas of growing up. Compare the female orgasm to a shallowly rooted tree which the wind may blow down more easily than its deeply rooted brother; it is still a tree, however, and if it can be sheltered and protected from storms that are too severe it can flower as beautifully as any other.

The fact that frigidity is so psychological, so subject to the mind, gives it almost a "willful" character. It is often as if a woman had "chosen" to be frigid in a very real sense. I don't mean consciously chosen to be, generally speaking. It's an unconscious choice. But the fact that it has that element of choosing in it often makes it a poignant condition indeed.

I know one case where the "choice" was, in part at least, conscious, and I am going to tell it briefly to emphasize my point, the fact that frigidity has a very high element of the mental as opposed to the biological.

Years ago, on a vacation with my husband, I met an older woman with whom, until her death, I had a very close and highly valued friendship. She was a wonderful woman. She was a doctor, but this had not prevented her from having five children of her own, two of whom have since become quite famous.

One day, after our friendship had deepened and we had begun to exchange confidences, she told me the following story. She had been deeply in love with her husband but had been totally frigid. This had not seemed strange at the time; she had been married in 1904, and the traditions of Victorianism were still very much adhered to. However, after the birth of her third child she began to experience some feelings of pleasure during intercourse, and these gradually increased. At this point she had her fourth child, and intercourse was interrupted for two or three months. When it was resumed her feelings of pleasure had increased enormously and on the second time she had a profound orgasm.

But she was not, like my actress, delighted with the new horizons the experience opened up for her. She was very consciously frightened and very consciously ashamed. All her background and training had been against it. She consciously decided never to let the experience repeat itself. She was entirely successful in her resolution, she told me. Unlike my actress, she threw off the lovely pink cloak of her feminine potentiality and never donned it again. Her husband had died after the birth of their last child, and it was not until a few years afterward, with the new information science had developed on the subject, that she realized the tragedy of her decision.

It's a poignant story, but I have not told it for that reason. I have told it because it illustrates very clearly how subject to the mind, to outside cultural and moral influences, feminine sexuality can be. If a grown woman can choose to destroy her mature and flowering sexuality at the height of its strength, just think of the fragility of this sexuality in the bud.

The Fear of Motherhood

On the whole, women will face anything to achieve motherhood. Recently a woman of thirty-five came to my office. She had called me twice to make appointments and twice broken them at the last moment. When this happens a psychiatrist will generally assume that the patient has become frightened of her decision to face up to whatever problem is troubling her and has gone into a last-minute flight. I had assumed that about this patient and had expected, if I ever did see her, to encounter a reticent, scared, perhaps terrified person.

Instead, the person who sat opposite me was a very pretty woman of thirty-five, well dressed, clear-eyed, and straightforward. She came right to the point.

"I'm here because I'm terrified of having children," she told me. "I must find out what's at the root of my fear."

"Was your fear the reason you canceled the two appointments?" I asked sympathetically.

"Oh no," she answered quickly, "the children were ill. We've had flu for a month. First one came down and then another."

"Children?" I asked in puzzlement. "What children?"

"Mine, of course," she said.

"How many do you have?" I asked.

"Four," she said, "but John and I want six and I

thought . . ." She paused; then, catching my smile, she looked down at the floor for a moment and back at me, and then we both burst into laughter.

She did have a fear of childbirth, however, dating from certain traumatic experiences in her childhood, and we were able to resolve it. It was a marked fear, but the important point is that even with it she had gone right on and had four children.

The maternal instinct is as deep and as ineradicable in women as the instinct to plant the seed of his species is in man. They both subserve the same ends, the continuation of the race, and even if a woman's childhood is sown with neurotic fears by unhappy parents—yes, even neurotic fears of childbirth—her desire to have children of her own will, in by far the majority of cases, survive relatively intact.

Thank heavens this is so. For the bearing and rearing of children are the beautiful destiny toward which a woman's whole body and personality point from earliest childhood on. If this profound goal cannot be achieved, the result is far too often a shriveling of the personality of the individual.

Thank heavens this is so, too, for the good of the race. I thought one of my colleagues expressed the whole thing very neatly in a paper given to a private psychiatric group recently. "If the feminists had been able to injure the maternal instinct of nineteenth-century woman to the same degree that they injured her sexual instinct, the Western world would by now be well on its way to being depopulated."

No, the maternal instinct cannot be fundamentally affected by adverse circumstances. However, the proper handling of information about the maternal instinct by a mother is very important to the proper sexual development of her daughter. Misunderstandings about maternity and what it means can scare a young child badly—so badly, in fact, that fear of it can be a direct cause of later frigidity.

Here's why the maternal instinct can cause trouble to a young girl's developing sexuality. Most women know this, even if they have never phrased it in this manner.

To gratify the maternal instinct a woman has to put her very life right on the line. In a real sense she has to be willing to say, and to keep on saying: "I am willing and ready to die for the sake of or the safety of my child."

I'm not only speaking of the now very slim chance that she might die in childbirth, though I should like to point out that until very recently that possibility had to be faced by every mother-to-be. And the enormously high mortality rate in childbirth throughout history and in every civilization shows very clearly that women *were* willing to face death to have their child. They have not changed.

What I mean more directly, however, is the fact that the maternal instinct demands of the woman in every situation an ever-readiness to put her child before herself, before her safety, before her personal needs, before everything.

Just yesterday I read of a woman who had saved two of her children from their burning home. The place had gone up like tinder and she had snatched them up, one seven and one ten, and, holding them under her arms, brought them to safety down a flaming stairway. She had thought her twelve-year-old had gotten out by himself but then discovered that he had not. She started back at once, without a moment's hesitation, to rescue him, but the building was now on the point of collapse and she was restrained by several firemen. However, so powerful was her drive to save her child that she broke away from their grasp and entered the building.

She found him, too, on the kitchen floor, overcome by smoke, and somehow got him to the front hall and out. She was badly burned, though she will live. But the child was all right; the child was all right! *That* was all that mattered.

And it is all that matters to every mother, unless, of course, she is dreadfully ill mentally—psychotic, in fact.

Just think of it; this aspect of the maternal instinct is more powerful than the instinct for self-preservation, which is known to be one of the basic instincts of all life. It supersedes self-preservation, annuls it; there are no reservations about it. It will never whisper: "You've done all you can; three powerful men are holding you down and you can't get to him anyway." It will fight powerfully and to the very end for the mother's right, her indomitable need, to save her child.

Of course most mothers never have to face physically dangerous situations for their children. In most lives the way this aspect of the mother instinct expresses itself is in everyday sacrifices. Mothers give up (and, in the healthy woman, with pleasure, by preference) their time, intellectual pursuits, careers, first to have the child and then to see him safely to maturity. Everything else a woman could call her own becomes secondary to this impulse in the maternal woman. As you saw in the normal woman, there are checks and balances within the female personality which prevent her from making a psychological martyr of herself to the point where she would be a *detriment* to her children, but at this time I should like to make a different point.

I have said that the maternal instinct is more powerful

than the instinct for self-preservation. I ask you to imagine for a moment how easily this characteristic of women could frighten a young girl if the experience of pregnancy or the role of the mother is presented to her in an improper way. She will react with acute anxiety, fear, rather than with joyful anticipation. This anxiety will color in dark hues though will not overwhelm her desire and determination to have babies. It *will* tend to take all the pleasure out of her sex life, however; it *will* tend strongly to make her frigid. And it will tend to make her a less effective mother, even a very poor one indeed.

The biological role of woman is motherhood. If a woman cannot dare to accept this aspect of her destiny, she will be deeply defeated in her life. From any standpoint one wishes to look at the maternal role, it is a great and beautiful one, embodying in it, and giving expression to qualities that are universally admired and cultivated: nobility, the sacrifice of self, fortitude, love that passeth understanding.

The depreciation of motherhood in any sense whatsoever in the mind of a young girl is a crime against her if one is in a position to be influential with her. To fill her with fears, misunderstandings, resentments of and reservations about her historic role is to cut her off from full flowering as a woman. The ability of woman to have an orgasm, her deepest form of relatedness to man, is planted rather lightly in biological soil, as we saw in the first section of this chapter. This ability is tightly interwoven with her psychological experiences at every stage of her development, and the quickest and most effective way to force her into frigidity is to teach her to be frightened of the maternal aspects of her personality.

We saw how well womankind functioned before the Industrial Revolution as an equal partner with her husband in the family home. Her experiences were fully satisfying to her body and mind because her role was recognized at its true value; she was needed, rewarded, depended upon, universally admired. When she lost her role and, in agony, mistakenly turned to feminism to find a new definition of self, or to Victorianism, she found only ashes, a depreciation of all those things that made her a woman; she found, and adopted, values that turned her against her feminine self, her maternal self, her passionate self. Scorn for true femininity was what she found and, tragically, she took this attitude for her own.

If woman is to find true happiness once again, she must return to her real and joyful self. She must relearn that surrender to her biological destiny is not a trap, not a condition of slavery to her uterus, of exploitation by man and nature, but rather a wonderful and privileged condition.

I should like to give the contents of a letter that came into my hands recently. I consider it a beautiful letter. It describes in a very simple way the reactions of a woman who had been caught in a maze of misunderstanding and fear but who had found her way out, had learned the power and joy she could receive by surrendering to her true destiny.

This letter was written by a young woman who had just become pregnant. Six months before, sick with anguish at her joyless marriage, unable to enjoy any aspect of her sexual relationship because of a constant and acute fear of becoming pregnant, she had consulted the pastor of her church, having heard that her church had psychiatric services. The pastor had gained her admission to a group-therapy project run by a psychologist. The group was made up of women who had encountered some difficulty in their lives with their husbands and children.

The patient had attended the group for four months and then had had to leave, for her husband's job had been transferred to another part of the state. The letter, sent to members of the group, arrived three months after her departure. I have received special permission from this ex-patient to reproduce this letter on the understanding that the names originally mentioned in it be changed.

Dear, dear Friends:

I will leave out all the details of our move here except to say that we are all settled down and in our wonderful new home. Anyway, I can't wait to tell you that I am going to have a baby. It is a constant astonishment to me, for it is so different from my expectations. It all happened so easily. I don't quite know how, but my fears and worries have left completely. I didn't know life could be like this. I must be a new person. If the doctor hadn't told me to stay relatively quiet I would be dancing in the streets. Sam says I sound like a honeymooner, but he's really delighted. To think what I have deprived both of us of because of a lot of nonsense!

The strangest thing is that I can't remember the things I used to talk about in the group. I wonder if this happens to everybody. I keep asking myself: What was so painful? What was it that made me always angry with Sam? And I've found a new deep love for my mother. I am not angry with her, only sorry that she had to miss so much. You probably won't remember, but when I asked my mother how she had felt when she was pregnant she had said quite sharply to me: "Put such thought out of your mind. You're young, so enjoy yourself. You'll know all about it soon enough, too soon." The reply seemed so ominous and foreboding to me. Plus the fact that she was constantly complaining about all things female. I guess I had picked up her attitude in toto without realizing it, until I aired the effects on me for the first time with all of you.

I tell you this so that you will know the fears *do* go when you are able to get them out and see them for what they are. I love you all, and I am deeply grateful to you, and I shall never, never forget the help my talk with all of you has given me.

> *With love and deep gratitude,*
> MARGARET

ANATOMY AND DESTINY

Chapter 7

ANATOMY AND DESTINY

We have seen two important reasons why women can, in the course of growing up, be deflected from true sexual maturity. Let us now look at a third, and equally important reason.

I have already described the so-called clitoridal woman to you, but now I must tell you more about the implications of her problem. You will remember that in the female genitalia both the clitoris and the vagina are capable of experiencing orgasm. This fact is of decisive importance to the problem of frigidity in women.

Why? It means, in effect, *that women have two distinct sexual organs, both capable of bringing her release from sexual tension*. In the unconscious sense many women can "choose" one type of sexual satisfaction in preference to another. This ability to choose often spells disaster, for one of these methods of gratification represents immaturity and is allied to neurosis.

A man has only one organ: his penis. He has been given no anatomical alternative. If, as happens in relatively rare cases, upsetting early experiences cause him to block off his sexual feelings, he simply becomes impotent. He will experience this impotency as a tremendous and tragic deprivation and will be powerfully motivated to overcome it. Those who have witnessed the sufferings of a man with such a problem will know just how powerful his drive back to health is.

The mature female's orgasm takes place within the vagina;

the fact that a woman can experience this kind of orgasm generally marks her as a fully developed woman in all aspects of her personality.

The clitoral orgasm takes place on the clitoris only. It excludes the vagina from sensual participation and it is often independent of the male penis. This kind of orgasm is possible at an early stage in female development. If, in growing up, the young girl becomes for any number of reasons frightened of mature vaginal sexuality, she can block that pathway and keep it blocked permanently without consciously experiencing any strong feelings of being deprived. She can do this because she is already having, as far as she knows, an amply satisfying experience through her clitoral orgasm. Since she has never experienced true sexual awakening, she doesn't know what she is missing, consequently she doesn't miss it.

You can see then that the woman who is able to have only a clitoral orgasm has no very strong motive for moving on to the next stage of sexual development. Her developing sexuality is channeled off into a sensual cul-de-sac and there, unless valiant and very conscious steps are taken, it tends to remain. As the early years of development move on into adolescence and further, the direction of her sexuality will not change, for she feels no reason to change it. Indeed the channel grows deeper, the earlier method of sexual response more ingrained. In the end she can respond in no other way.

Since such a woman is not advancing sexually she tends, too, to remain static emotionally. If her psychological fears of real womanhood are not resolved, she now begins to build up defenses of her childish emotional needs and of her childish methods of sexual gratification. By the time she is ready, in terms of her age, for marriage, she may very well have a full-blown neurosis that militates gravely against the success of any close relationship.

This then, is how biology can represent destiny, with a helping hand from psychology. In a very real sense this dual potentiality of woman's anatomy contains the seeds of sexual and hence personal tragedy.

Remember that the woman whose orgasm is confined to the clitoris is definitely frigid. Statistics on the prevalence of this kind of sexual problem are not available, but most psychiatrists and psychoanalysts agree that it is very widespread, may even be the dominant form of frigidity in our society.

Unhappily many women who suffer from this form of frigidity have not been helped in the past several years by widely published and thoroughly erroneous views concerning sexual behavior in the human female. The Kinsey report, above all, has erred in this respect. It makes no differentiation between vaginal and clitoral orgasm. Indeed its authors passionately defend the view that all orgasm is clitoral. How trained observers could come to this conclusion, it is difficult to say. The great observers in the field of human sexuality in the past fifty years have been in the field of psychiatry. They have been and are unanimous in their observation on the difference between clitoral and vaginal orgasm and its importance to personality development and to neurosis. The fact that the Kinsey report ignores this important and well-established fact about the female sex and, even worse, defends the opposite viewpoint simply invalidates, from psychiatry's viewpoint, many of its basic findings about orgasm.

The sad thing, however, is that the Kinsey report is often used to bolster the neurotically defensive attitude of women who are able to achieve only clitoral orgasm. They can say to themselves that their method of gratification is perfectly normal; do they not have a tremendous body of "scientific" data to support their view? And somehow or other women with this difficulty do get hold of the Kinsey "results." I myself have had several women suffering from the kind of problem I have just described quote Kinsey to me at some length in defense of their method of gratification. And, having checked with several of my colleagues, I find that they all report many similar experiences.

This is unfortunate. Women who suffer from any other form of frigidity are frequently motivated to face up to their problem by feelings of sexual frustration. Sooner or later, driven by natural hungers, they will take steps to throw off the yoke of their difficulty.

The woman who is able to have a clitoral orgasm, however, has no such strong motivation. She can ruin her life and never be the wiser, never realize the reason why.

I strongly advise, therefore, that such women be more than usually wary about their tendency to be complacent, more than usually insistent about finding a way out of their dilemma; above all, they must recognize their life situation *as* a dilemma, a serious one that can far too easily be rationalized.

At this point, then, I wish to emphasize once more the role of woman's responsibility in this matter of sexual response. There is often a stronger-than-usual underlying irrational fear in clitoridal women which makes them hesitate, even when they have admitted their problem, to face up to it in any effective way. I wish therefore to reiterate the point that nobody who suffers from this problem should feel shame or blame for it. You did not choose in any conscious sense to remain on this earlier and less "dangerous" plane of sexual development. Your body made the choice, if you will, but you had nothing to say about that. The strange dual sexuality of woman is at the base of the matter. It all happened because you misunderstood or misinterpreted certain early experiences. Or a grownup responsible for your very early training was ignorant or misinformed.

But now it will be the better part of wisdom and valor for you to face up to the fact that your method of gratification is an expression of immaturity, even if that immaturity was forced upon you when you were too young to know the difference. Don't subside into feelings of guilt and inferiority about the problem. Remember that you are not alone. There are probably millions of women who have the same problem. You can be one who achieves the joys that lie just beyond this. They are real and solid joys, and they contain none of the terrors you had thought they contained. Not one.

One of the things I have found helpful in motivating a woman with a clitoridal problem is to face her with its effect on her husband. Women with this fixation have a curious inability to see these effects or to face up to them realistically. I have found that even when such women know that their form of gratification is infantile and expressive of neurosis they insist that their husbands not only do not mind the manual manipulation necessary to bring them to climax but actually prefer this method of sexual contact to intercourse.

Such has never been the case in my years of clinical experience. Husbands mind very much indeed.

Here, very recently, is what one husband, whose wife has been able to move on from her clitorial fixation, told me: "I feel like a man again. No matter what anybody says, your wife's response is the most important thing, and it's got to be a response *in* intercourse. If she doesn't respond that way, you gradually lose faith in yourself and then you lose interest in making love."

Another man, whose wife has just come to me and who has never been able to have an orgasm except clitorally, recently said: "I may sound unsympathetic and petty, but if I felt there was no end in sight to this kid stuff, I mean this form of having to stroke endlessly, I think I'd give up on the sex part. It's lost all its fun."

He'll get his fun back, for his wife, knowing a lot more than she did when she started, is very intent on helping herself. And the husband is *not* unsympathetic or petty in his complaints. He is simply human, and there's a limit to human endurance.

The wife's denial that the husband is bothered by a clitoridal problem, I have found, is based on a deeper fear—the fear that the marriage is being endangered by her problem. Both of the women mentioned above (and many others I have treated) finally admitted that they had come for help because of their fear that their marriage was headed for trouble, that their husbands were close to leaving them. The fact is, though, that many men seem to have a very high tolerance for this problem in their wives. I have yet to find any man who has broken up his marriage for that reason. Indeed both the men I have quoted above had reassured me that they could and would go on taking their frustrations. They just strongly preferred not to.

No, the danger is not from the husband. Real men rarely leave women for that reason. The danger is from the woman herself. She it is who, because of her immaturity, will do the rejecting rather than face her problem. The real danger is that she will force the man away from her without even realizing that she has done so.

You begin to see, then, that the chief characteristic of women with this type of problem is evasiveness, hiding from the facts. It is as if they feared what they would find out if they faced up to things. I can only tell them that they are not going to find out a thing that is really frightening, not a thing that they cannot handle.

And I should like to put the mind of all such women to rest on one particular point. I cannot count the number of times that women with a clitoridal problem have asked me whether I believed that, just under the surface, they had a homosexual problem or at least strong homosexual inclinations. The answer is invariably no.

Let me give you an example of one such typical case. Not long ago a young nurse came to see me. She was extremely upset and wept copiously before she could bring herself to tell me her problem. She had been married for about a year and had found that she could not have an orgasm during intercourse. It was necessary for her husband to manipulate her clitoris for a rather extended period of time before she could come to a climax. After she told me this she remained silent for a long time. Then she burst out with it. "Doctor, I think I'm homosexual."

"Why?" I asked.

"Well, I had this dream, and I was hugging the head nurse in the hospital and I felt very warm and good inside."

"Any other damning evidence?" I asked.

Now she really blushed. She hung her head, and one could hardly keep from going over and patting her head and saying there, there. "Yes," she said. "When I was twelve. With this other girl. We used to, used to . . ." Words failed her.

"Play with each other sexually?" I asked as gently as possible.

She looked at me, wide-eyed and said, "Yes," nodding tragically.

She had had no repetition of the experience since she had really grown up, and I was able to set her mind completely at rest on that matter. She was not at all homosexual. That symptom is a very severe one, of course, and not always amenable to treatment. It always implies that the woman prefers women to men; she falls in love with objects of the same sex. She has no conscious interest in men sexually.

Our little nurse's "homosexual" dream simply meant that she was having a disturbing time with her husband sexually and wanted a "mother image" to protect her from her difficulties, help her through them. She got one in me, of course, and her need for such a mother was probably why she selected a woman psychiatrist in the first place.

Her early sexual play with another little girl is perfectly normal. Not all children indulge in this kind of play, but many do, and unless it continues into adolescence it is generally harmless.

The reasons behind this delusion of homosexuality are complex. They lie in an early confusion of the clitoris with the male penis, as I will illustrate later. But you may be certain of one thing—you are not going to discover that your problem is based on homosexuality as it appears in the difficulty called "lesbianism." To hold onto such mistaken conceptions is to frighten oneself with self-told ghost stories after the fashion of young children.

I wish here to cover just one more attribute of the woman whose sexual feelings have become fixed on her clitoris, one which, if she is forewarned, she will and should be suspicious of. It is the tendency to look for solutions for her problem in directions where no solutions lie.

I have treated women who have tried everything under the

sun in their search for an easy resolution of their clitoridal problem—drugs, surgery, even yoga. One of the most widely used evasions can be found (and how often it is!) in the many popular manuals written, ostensibly, to tell one how to achieve a happy marriage. Such books, for the most part published in all good faith, almost invariably counsel married partners to diversify their sexual positions during intercourse. Many of these books contain illustrations to drive their lesson home.

There is nothing wrong with this advice in and of itself. Anybody with a modicum of experience knows that variety is one of the finest spices of love. The books generally, if not always, neglect to say, however, that such variety is only relevant to a sex life in which the partners have no deep-seated sexual problem to start with. By omitting that piece of information these books give the strong tacit impression that variety of sexual position will solve an already well-established sexual difficulty.

The desperate woman will seize upon these implications as upon a panacea for her ills. I must state here that all of the innumerable positions of love described in the Hindu Kamasutra (from which so many of our marriage manuals, incidentally, derive much of their information) will not undo a clitoral fixation. A woman is asking for just one more emotional defeat if she insists that a solution lies in this direction.

We have now seen the three things that make frigidity possible in women. I will repeat them briefly so that you'll remember them later.

The first is the fact that the female orgasm is not a biological necessity in woman as it is in man. The race can and does go on if women fail to have full sexual satisfaction. This strongly suggests why the female orgasm is so susceptible to psychological influences of an adverse kind.

The second is the fact that motherhood calls for tremendous psychological and sometimes physical sacrifices; it means that a woman has to reverse the natural law of self-preservation and put her children's welfare ahead of her own. This is deeply frightening to some women and, unless they are properly educated, can cause them to fear their feminine sexual impulse to the point where they are unable to enjoy love-making.

The third reason is that women have, in effect, two organs of gratification, the clitoris and the vagina. Clitoral orgasm is immature, evades true feminine sexuality, and is considered a form of frigidity. However, millions of women find this earlier method of gratification so satisfying that they are not motivated to move up to the mature level.

Chapter 8

THE GROWTH OF LOVE

In medical school one of our courses included the study of the psychological stages of development man goes through from infancy to maturity. It also included the various pitfalls people encounter during these stages, the biological and psychological experiences that can prevent them from reaching psychological maturity.

During one class in which we reviewed the psychological hazards of adolescence a very intelligent student raised his hand and was recognized by the professor. "How does anyone *ever* really grow up?" this student asked.

The class laughed, of course. But the professor, after the laughter had died down, took the question quite seriously and complimented the student for his acuity. He then proceeded to address us for a half hour on the indomitable and surging drive of the human body and mind toward health and pleasure, a drive that will often overcome seemingly insurmountable obstacles, that will pause for a while at times, apparently defeated, only to revive its original energy and resume its move toward the goal of health and maturity.

We see this drive daily in people who come for psychiatric help, and we know that it is the single most important element in psychological healing. As soon as the difficulty which was holding the person back has been resolved, his whole mind and body tend once again to resume their move toward health and happiness. It is well to keep this factor in mind as we explore here the stages of development women go through on their way to grown-uphood.

We have seen the grown-up, truly feminine woman in operation. You wil. remember that she is a delighted and delightful partner in that closest and most perfect expression of love, the sexual act. You will recall that a great part of her personality is organized around her maternal instinct and that the chief characteristic of that instinct is a pleasure in giving, an unappeasable altruism that always puts husband and child before self, even to the point of risking her own life and welfare. Her central activities revolve around her nest building and child rearing. Her personality is characterized by a deep intuitiveness about others. She is inward and passive, her energies devoted to that deepest of all needs, the procreation of the race of man through her own body. Her husband, by contrast, is aggressive, occupied basically with his struggles in the outside world. Her stage, the focus of her central interest, is the home and its preservation and its happiness.

How did she get this way? Or, in the case of women who fail to achieve a truly feminine personality, what actually happens, how do they get *that* way?

To be able to answer these questions, one must first understand the stages of development that women, all women, go through in the process of growing up. These phases of development have been under the closest scientific scrutiny for several decades. The realization of their importance for psychological health and illness has been one of the major achievements of modern psychiatry. They have been thoroughly explored, and if we do not yet know all there is to know about the subject, we still know a great deal.

The material I am about to go into is fact, scientific fact, not opinion. If the information here seems new or strange or even irritating to you, do not be surprised or upset. It is new and strange to most people and at first it may not seem applicable to you. But if you will stay with it, use it to understand the case histories which I will discuss afterward, you will gradually see why understanding these phases is so necessary and helpful to the individual who has not yet been able to achieve her full femininity. As you have been told many times, all psychological problems are rooted in infancy, childhood, or in adolescence. To uproot these problems, we must return to those stages of development with new tools, new ideas, a new master plan.

There are two over-all stages of biological and psychological development that every individual must go through. The first stage lasts from birth to about ten years of age. In turn this stage is divided into two phases; the first, the phase we call infancy, lasts roughly for the first five years of life. The second phase we call the latency period and occupies the second five years of life.

The first five years of growth, the infantile period, is of enormous importance for later development. In this phase the whole personality takes the shape and develops the characteristics that will distinguish it from that time on.

At this point I have to note a certain scientific fact that may surprise or disconcert you. I ask you to withhold any prejudices of a personal or moral kind you may have about this fact, for they will only obscure the entire issue and make it difficult for you to understand one of the most important contributions science has made to the understanding of the human mind.

The decisive fact, then, about the infantile period is that the little creature is very heavily endowed with strong sexual feelings. The students of this subject are in absolute agreement on this point. There is no longer the slightest inkling of a doubt about it. All scientific methods of checking the fact have been employed. These range from direct observation of children to the recovery of childhood memories through hypnosis or while subjects have been under the influence of hypnotic drugs, direct reports from children, and several other sources.

This sexual drive is centered on the genitals from the outset, and it can be seen very clearly in children who masturbate. Such masturbation is a perfectly normal activity in boys and girls during this entire period.

The important point about this masturbation is the fact that the little girl masturbates by the manipulation of her clitoris. She has no awareness of her vagina as a sensual area.

The sexual feelings of infancy increase in intensity after the second or third year. Now masturbation may increase. In a very real sense the strong sensual feelings experienced at this age set the mold for the later sexual development of the child.

For the first three years the little girl is deeply and primarily attached to her mother. In the sense that infants "realize" things, the little girl knows that her mother is the source of all her security. These feelings have a very clear sensual nature. The little girl loves to be close to the mother, to be stroked by her, to have her mother clean her genitalia, etc. She associates her masturbation with the pleasant sensations she receives, psychologically and physically, from her mother.

Around three years of age the little girl becomes aware of her growing attachment to her father. His tenderness toward her and his play with her stimulate her whole being, and her sensuality becomes increasingly attached to him. At first she is not aware of the conflict in this attachment, but as her little mind becomes a bit more aware of reality she senses, however vaguely and incompletely, the fact that her increasingly sensual response to her father has put her into competition with her mother; another woman has a prior claim on her first man! At this point she begins to develop hostile feelings toward her mother.

The whole thing seems too fantastic! A little child competing with her mother for her father's love? Impossible!

But let me give you a very clear example of a typical dream my women patients have. This is the dream of a frigid woman who had had several consultations with me and in one of them, the day before the dream, suddenly remembered that at the age of five she had been absolutely convinced that her father would marry her when she grew up. She had buried that memory in her mind, only to resurrect it in therapy.

Her dream, then, was that she was lying in a crib. A tall thin man with glasses and a thin mustache was lying on a bed nearby. A stout, florid-faced woman lay next to him. Suddenly this woman had a convulsive seizure and, after a few moments of writhing, became still. The man then looked at her and smiled as if pleased. "She's dead," he said. Then he rose from the bed, went to the crib, and picked my patient up. "We will have four," he said to her, and she felt immeasurably excited and pleased.

My patient woke in a great state of anxiety. In our session she told me that her father had been tall, thin, and sometimes wore glasses to read in bed. And her mother was stout and very high-colored. My patient then suddenly recalled that in the childhood fantasy of marriage to her father she had decided that she would have four children with him. Her logic was this: her mother had had three children; she would go her mother one better!

I cannot tell you how often we psychiatrists get, directly from our patients, information as clearly confirmatory as this of the existence of an early triangle between mother, father, and child. It causes a conflict in the child, of course, and this early conflict in the little girl takes place in a very subtle manner, so subtle, indeed, that its very existence escaped the conscious notice of mankind from the dawn of history until the end of the nineteenth century. Just before the turn of the twentieth century Sigmund Freud, then an obscure Viennese psychiatrist, while using hypnosis on patients suffering from powerful feelings of repressed guilt, noted that these feelings were always connected with very early sexual conflicts. He was astonished to discover that these sexual conflicts dated back to early childhood, and in case after case he was able to demonstrate not only that children possessed strong sensual feelings but that these feelings became attached first to the mother and then to the father, causing a conflict in the childish mind which had to be resolved, He called this the Oedipal situation. If it was not resolved, the child developed irrational feelings of guilt which could and did impede normal sexual and psychological growth.

I described this early source of conflict to a woman patient of mine recently in much the same way that I have described it here. After pondering for a moment she asked a question that goes to the heart of the matter. "If this early situation causes a conflict in the child which can lead to a neurosis later, why did nature design things that way? I thought nature set things up to foster growth, not to hinder it."

The observation and question were fine ones and raised points that are generally ignored. Nature *did* design this early sexual conflict for a very special reason. She did it to foster the growth of the little girl, to push her on to the next step in the development of her femininity, to move her a little farther along the path to her ultimate role of wife and mother.

Let me explain this a bit further. For the first few years by the very nature of family life, as we have seen, all the little girl's feelings are focused on her mother. She is the center, the fountain of life itself; the little one looks to her for food, security on all levels, and "love." This love soon becomes tinged with a very strong erotic feeling connected with the little one's growing sensuality, which, as we have seen, is centered on her clitoris.

Now, it is necessary for humans to love and to have erotic feelings centered on others. But clearly, if this early love situation did not change at some point, the little girl would grow up to have women as her erotic centers of interest. Nature intends no such end result. She intends these erotic feelings to become ultimately very much man-centered. Thus she makes the role of the father in the child's development all-important. He becomes the first bridge from the infantile erotic and dependent relationship with the mother to mature relationships with members of the opposite sex. There are, of course, several other bridges that the growing girl will have to traverse on her journey to maturity, but this first one is of central importance. Ultimately, of course, she will have to give up her father, too, as the center of erotic interest, but he will remain in her unconscious life as the model of all that she wants from the male in her life.

We see, then, at the end of this early phase of development the first big step in the preparation of the little girl for her ultimate destiny as wife and mother. But since we know that she is nowhere near ready for such functions we might wonder how nature ends this early period and enters the second important period of growth.

The end of the first stage and the beginning of the second (which, you will recall, will last to about ten years of age) begins with a remarkable psychological event: the early infantile sexuality goes completely underground. The little girl "forgets" that she ever went through such sensual experiences, that there was anything the least bit erotic in her former attachments. Her masturbation stops, under normal circumstances, and she enters into approximately a five-year period of total non-sexuality.

However, you must understand that when I use the word "forget" I do not mean it literally. In psychiatry we use the word "repression" to describe this kind of forgetting. It means the ability of the human mind to push anything it does not wish to recall out of awareness, into a part of the mind called the unconscious. When we repress something, a memory or experience, we do not remember that it ever happened with our conscious mind. However, it remains quite intact in our unconscious mind and can and does exert an influence upon us that we are not aware of. Too, it can be revived in the conscious mind by later experiences, or, even if it does not revive, later experiences can be very much influenced by the "forgotten" memory.

The new stage into which the young girl now enters is called the "latency period," because the sexual feelings of the earlier period have become repressed, or latent.

The latency period is chiefly characterized by an attempt on the part of the little girl to understand and master her environment. It is marked by a tremendous growth physically and mentally. She is interested in everything, in everything that gives her a chance to advance herself physically: rope-jumping, doll-playing, ball-playing, swimming, climbing, running; there is sometimes very little that she does, feels, or thinks in this period that distinguishes her in any very important manner from a little boy of the same age. She may be a bit more obedient, a bit better about doing her homework than a boy, but not dramatically so.

We may ask, then, what nature's intention in bringing on this latency period might be? Let me put it this way. Nature, plainly and simply, wishes to give the child a chance to grow a little mentally, to learn to master her body and mind, to integrate the earlier phase of development, to learn to form personal relationships so that when she comes to the next great step in development, the phase marked by menstruation and female maturation, she will be ready. Think what what would happen if the little girl were plunged from the stresses and strains of infantile sexuality directly into full sexual readiness. Her body might be ready, but psychologically she would have no understanding of her environment, no idea of personal relationships, no sense of her self or of her abilities. She would have, as the actress Elizabeth Taylor noted of herself and her reaction to a too-early plunge into grown-up experiences, "a child's mind in a woman's body." Nature *intends* no such dilemma for women. She has a step-by-step plan which leads the woman, if parents co-operate, safely to the haven of physical *and* psychological maturity.

The latency period is also marked by a very close relationship to the parents, particularly to the father. However, there are now no conscious sexual feelings attached to him. She admires and values her father above all other things and wants his admiration and very high regard too. Most fathers instinctively give their little daughters a great deal of love and reassurance during this phase, and the child basks in it as a flower in the sun. She strives to do the things that will please him, make him notice her, make him love her. His responses are studied assiduously, and it is in this way that she receives her first real experience with the all-important feminine need to "please her man." The feelings of joy she gets from his pleasure in her accomplishments, physical and mental, are the precursors of the rewards she will later prize so highly when bestowed on her by a loving husband. As you might suspect, this period is very important to her development into full womanhood with its varied psychological give-and-take. If the father seriously fails in his role during this period he can do irreparable harm to the growing girl.

The mother's role, of course, continues to be important too. The little girl has repressed her guilt feelings toward her mother, along with all of her directly sensual feelings, and during the latency period Mother emerges as a model to imitate. In effect the little girl says something like this to herself: "She, after all, got the man I prize most highly in the whole world. Therefore, she must have something very desirable. Therefore, I'll imitate it." She proceeds to do just that.

Of course I do not mean that this is *all* there is to her feelings about her mother; she loves her mother deeply and abidingly and without her would feel, and indeed would be bereft. Her imitation of her mother is a tribute to those feelings too. However, I may remind you that I am selecting those aspects of the child's relationships that bear directly on her later sexual maturity.

The next stage of development starts approximately at the age of ten and ends with the complete maturation, psychological and biological, of the individual woman. It is often divided into two phases; the first phase, which lasts until thirteen, fourteen, or fifteen, we call puberty; the second, by that much-misunderstood word "adolescence."

Puberty is ushered in by great glandular changes in the child. The young body begins to take on the semblance of womanhood. Breasts begin to grow; pubic hair starts. Gradually the uterus, or womb, stirs, begins to expand, readies itself to hold the child which will ultimately grow there. In the midst of this preparatory growth menstruation, the cyclical ebb and flow of fecund woman, starts in earnest. In a few months the child stands just within the portal of physical maturity.

The little girl now again (for the first time since infancy) begins to experience rather strong sexual feelings, and she reacts to them with some anxiety. She may start once more to masturbate clitorally, although this time the act is accompanied by guilt feelings and with apprehension. As I have pointed out, these feelings of apprehension can be thought of as fully justified. Her sexuality is going to lead to motherhood, and this in turn means that she is going to have to face the dangers of pregnancy and childbirth, the biological need of putting her child's welfare ahead of her own. In effect, as we have seen, she is going to suspend the law of self-preservation as it applies to her own person.

The little girl knows this; she knows it with her body and mind, for even the most prudishly reared child cannot be prevented from finding out the facts of life. If her parents have not told her she will soon find out all there is to know from her girl friends.

I have said that the new changes in her cause her apprehension. They also cause her feelings of joy, excitement, and intense curiosity. Throughout her entire puberty she will run between these two states of mind, anxiety on the one hand and feelings of pleasure on the other. At times she will look back in envy at the blissful latency period when she was not bothered by these powerful indications of her biological destiny, which lies immediately ahead. She will hate her developing breasts, her menstrual period, the hair growing under her arms and around her genitalia. At other moments she will be rapturous about these very same changes.

At this point she withdraws from her parents to a large extent. Nature, as we saw in the latency period, must not only prepare her biologically for womanhood but must ready her psychologically too. If the little girl were to maintain the total dependency on her parents that she has had up to this point in her growth, she would not be able to develop the fullness of personality, the strength and individuality necessary for successful wifehood and motherhood.

But she is not a woman yet by any means. Do not get that impression, for there are vital steps ahead which she must take first. The attempt some girls make to embrace true sexuality and feminine functioning around the age of fourteen or fifteen is generally disastrous. In normal development she will flutter between strong feelings of dependency on her parents and rebellion against them, or rather rebellion against her intense desire to be a little girl with them again. The success of this phase of her growth is marked by achieving the feeling that she has the "potentiality," *not* the actuality, of freedom from her parents.

At some point during this period she will become dramatically attached to a girl friend. This fact is so unalterable in normal development that the whole period of puberty is often referred to as "the chum stage" of development. She uses this friend to buttress her feelings of separateness, of independence from the parents. The two share secrets together constantly, pool their information on all matters pertaining to sex, boys, women, childbirth. The friendship is a liberal education for both and should be encouraged for the most part. The girl friend is sometimes older by a year or two or three, and the younger one's worship of her is clearly a substitute for her feelings toward her own mother. If the older girl is not too precocious sexually, nothing but good can come from this relationship.

Very gradually puberty merges into adolescence. This is the last stage before maturity. I call this whole period the "daydream stage." It is a period of almost literal waking dreams on the part of the young lady. She is still held lightly by the long preparatory sleep of childhood and early youth, but she is ready to wake. Her head is filled with tremendous plans for herself. These plans usually have a highly maternal and altruistic character about them; she will become a great doctor and serve suffering humanity in darkest Africa, or she will become a lawyer and defend the poor free of charge, or she will become a nurse and, under fire that would daunt a lesser creature, she will tend the wounded among our boys at the front. She has scores of great loves with boys or men whom she considers wonderful—all in her head.

The satisfaction of her now nearly mature maternal and sexual impulses through such dreams is clear. But they serve another function which is perhaps a bit more obscure. She is not quite ready for real love yet. She has still half a foot in childhood, is still reluctant to give herself wholly to the realities of grown-uphood. She needs to hang upon the tree, so to speak, for a few more years, to ripen a bit. The great roles she plays in her daydreams are, in most cases, not achievable. They allow her, by the very impossibility of their fruition, to have her cake and eat it too.

Yes, the dream of young love is a long and lovely one, and it readies the dreamer for real love. Woman will always be a romantic dreamer, a weaver of inner reveries, of tapestries of thought that give her whole personality its richness and flavor. In love, as in life, man is a doer, an aggressive achiever. Woman is the passive one; she is the dreamer who values the man's achievements, who creates the need for his achievement and gives color and glory to it through her appreciation of it. The dreams of adolescence ready her for this role with her man.

Adolescence is a gradual preparation for true sexuality and love. In it the young girl conquers her impulse to masturbate, though in certain rather "free" communities there may be a great deal of petting with the opposite sex. If the girl's development is normal and she puts the normally high value on herself that is characteristic of this period, she will not have sexual intercourse until she actually falls in love seriously. Also, nature gives her an almost unerring instinct for the "right" man, one who will cherish her and their children.

It is important to know that it is the man who ultimately wakens the sleeping beauty sexually. Until she is ready for intercourse and all that it implies in the way of a relationship, she is conscious of no particularly urgent vaginal sensations of a sexual nature. The man awakens these for the first time in the act of love.

With her first intercourse, she finds a whole continent of sensations whose existence she had only heard about second-hand. While her clitoral sensations may still be quite pleasurable in the period of foreplay, her whole body now, in excitement, soon learns to yearn for the penetration of her lover's penis, the unspeakable delight of the now vaginally centered sensations he can give her. She has little or no block to these sensations; there may be a period of adjustment for a few weeks or months until they become totally unfettered from childhood inhibitions and fears, but the months will be short. Now true orgasm is hers at virtually every sexual encounter with her husband, and in mutual delight their relationship will prosper and deepen.

Chapter 9

DANGERS ON THE ROAD TO WOMANHOOD

Now we have seen the stages the normal woman goes through on her way to true sexual and psychological maturity, the step-by-step process of her growth. But we must, of course, ask what might happen to impede this growth, what pitfalls lie along the way into which she may stumble (or be pushed), causing her to develop symptoms of frigidity and the personality difficulties that always accompany this frigidity.

I should like to list these pitfalls in the same manner that I showed the normal and unimpeded growth of a woman: by taking the stages of development in the order of their appearance. If you are able to see the specific dangers along the path to grown-uphood, you may avoid repeating them with your own child and may learn much about the origins of your own problem, particularly as I show their application in the specific case histories that follow this chapter.

In the first or infantile stage of development the greatest danger to the child comes from ignorance on the part of the parents. In the past, parents did not know that the newborn babe has sensual feelings that become quite specific by the time he or she is three years of age and continue that way until he is about six. I am afraid many parents still do not know this fact, either have not heard of it or do not believe it is true.

Such a lack of knowledge is often accompanied by a moral horror of masturbation or, at the very least, of strong feelings of moral disapproval. This often leads the parent, especially the mother, to restrain the child from such sensual activity. Many parents slap the infant's hands, some systematically remove the child's hands when they see her playing with herself. Others, when the child learns to speak, will reprove her for her activities, often spank her if the activity persists.

Such an attitude could not be more mistaken and can have a disastrous effect on the child. The infant is tremendously responsive to even the subtlest disapproval on the part of the parents. In this all-important area she will react violently to punishment and even to verbal warnings. Often she will not only attempt to prevent her own masturbatory activity but will try to repress the whole of her sexual nature in an effort to keep her mother's love. She may be quite successful in doing this, kill all her natural impulses in the bud. First experiences, as we know, are of great importance in development, and this early inhibition of her sexual nature can, and often does, lay the groundwork for sexual frigidity and a generally inhibited and circumscribed personality.

Another danger in this period can come from an exorbitant amount of overt love from the father. This is very difficult for certain men to understand fully. They argue, and quite cogently, that the young need a great deal of love, demonstrative love. That is indeed so, but it must also be remembered that children at this age are extremely erotic. They can be overstimulated sensually if the father does not bestow his loving caresses in judicious amounts, and the result can be a strong fixation of erotic feelings on the father, with a consequent overload of guilt feelings. These guilt feelings can lead to total frigidity in later life, and indeed may be the leading cause of this symptom, as we shall presently see. I am not saying that a father should not caress and dandle his little daughter; that would be against nature. He should, however, dole out his physical expressions of love in amounts that are not too stimulating to the child.

Another pitfall the child can encounter at this stage is quite the opposite in nature. It is, luckily, met with infrequently, but it does happen and it can have an important effect on the child's development. I am speaking of seduction by an older child or an adult. It is not unknown for nurse maids or even older brothers and sisters to stroke the young child's genitals. German and Austrian maids used to do it as a matter of course, stroking the little boy's testicles and penis or the little girl's vulva to put the child to sleep. However, this is absolutely harmful to the child, causing an overexcitation that can have a permanent effect on her sexuality. Masturbation is normal for this age, and in this form of narcissistic sexual activity the child is able to control the amount of sexual excitation she receives. Under normal circumstances she will not exceed this amount. However, stimuli from the outside are *not* self-regulating, and the child's ego is not sufficiently mature to handle this overexcitation.

The result of a seduction on the child at this age can be disastrous. It can lead to any of the major forms or degrees of frigidity. In my experience, however, it most frequently seems to lead to the form known as "psychic frigidity."

I might add that the same general effect can be caused by certain local irritations of the little girl's genitalia. These can be easily recognized. The itching and soreness of such irritations may cause the child to scratch or stroke her genitals excessively, and this too may occasion an overexcitation which the little ego is not yet ready to handle. Or it may cause the child to associate pleasurable sensations with painful sensations, and this association may cause difficulties of a psychological nature later. Only real ignorance on the part of the parent could allow such easily remedied conditions to persist to the point where they might do harm to the child. On the other hand, I do not wish to alarm parents unnecessarily or to cause any mother to become obsessively concerned about the frequent irritations children may get in the genital area. To cause any real harm to the child psychologically, such irritations must be chronic and unattended to for a long period. The usual short-term irritation has no known permanent effect on the child's development psychologically.

The last major danger of this early period which I shall mention stems from any deep-seated emotional problem of the mother. If because of problems created in *her* childhood the mother either neglects or overprotects the child to a great extent or over a long period of time, there can be serious harm done to the development of the little one. Overprotection can destroy the self-reliance of the child, keep her from passing into the rewarding and growth-provoking relationship with her father which moves her into the next natural step in development. Neglect, on the other hand, can thrust her into too close an association with the father and have equally dire results.

Failure of the relationship with her father is the chief danger the little girl faces during her latency period, which, as you may recall, she encounters from six to ten years of age. She has transferred many of the feelings of love and dependency, which a few years before she had felt for her mother, to this new idol. Forever after he will be the model male in her life, though she will seek her ideal in other men. For the present she worships him, and his approval means more to her than anything else in the world.

If the father is a disapproving and critical man and directs such attitudes toward his daughter, she may develop strong feelings of inferiority. These can lead her to feel that men are virtually impossible to please, and she can thus become fearful of them, feeling that if a man finds out her true nature he will disapprove of it. No reality or later acceptance by a man will overcome this irrational conviction unless, when she is grown, a woman with such a self-attitude examines herself deeply and eradicates this mistaken conception of the male. Her feelings of inferiority extend to her sexual drive, which she is apt to repress, as if it were discreditable, like the rest of her personality.

Some fathers, of course, have a closer identification with their sons than with their daughters. Men who are not aware of this tendency to wreak great havoc with a daughter's personality at this stage of her growth. Since she adores her father and wishes to become what he will admire, she will quickly detect her father's preference for the male. This often causes her to attempt to cultivate male characteristics and male pursuits and to depreciate totally all those typically feminine goals which one day she must achieve if she is to be a true woman.

The latency period, as we saw, is a non-sexual time for both boys and girls. Aside from their anatomical structure, there is little difference between boys and girls at this juncture: their glands function in roughly the same way; none of the typical characteristics which will differentiate them later have yet appeared. They are both interested in mastering the world about them and the world inside them; they are both roughly equal as far as their innate store of aggressiveness is concerned. Indeed, many scientists call this whole period the bisexual period of development.

For these reasons a father who implants male goals into his daughter's psyche at this point finds a ready audience. Psychoanalysis shows us that the little girl very often can develop fantasies of an extremely odd kind at this juncture. In some children, for example, the idea that they can somehow magically grow a penis and turn into a boy is too often quite conscious. But even if such ideas do not become conscious, the yearning of the little girl to become a boy to win her father's esteem can remain as part of the total equipment of her unconscious mind. Later, although hidden and disguised, this wish can be at the root of much of her sexual problems with men, causing her to be neurotically competitive with them and to reject her own female role as unworthy.

We saw that the girl in puberty and in adolescence had a formidable task to achieve. She must learn to accept and to love the "dangerous" role of the woman—she must, in effect, be willing to reverse the natural law of self-preservation and put childbirth and the welfare of the child ahead of her own needs and safety.

If she is not encouraged to believe that the feminine role is a worthy one, if she is taught that the male role is superior, then she will be highly motivated to reject her femininity and, almost literally, try to be a boy. It is frequently exactly this that occurs when a woman's fear and rejection of femininity result in an inability to respond vaginally in sexual intercourse. In a curious and of course unconscious manner she may hold onto the sensual responses of her clitoris as if she had a small penis, but feel unable to allow the sensual feelings to be experienced within the vagina.

The young girl may be influenced to reject her feminine role by the mother as well as by the father. If the mother herself has a strong resentment of her own femininity and, like so many women, has been reared to feel that the role of wife and mother is a degraded and worthless one, she can pass this attitude on to her daughter without speaking a word. The child sees it in her mother's reactions to her father in everyday life, hears it in her complaints, and sometimes feels it in the resigned and hopeless attitude with which she may face her life.

When I emphasize this early "masculine" direction which a little girl's values may be given, I do not wish to confuse the reader. There is a "tomboy" stage through which many girls pass. This is a perfectly natural phase in her development and has nothing to do with the problem unless the child holds onto her tomboyism until well after twelve years of age. This natural emulation of little boys is really quite a feminine gesture on the little girl's part—she is trying to learn more about what that wonderful opposite sex does and thinks and feels. In this way she enters into her first friendly relationships with males other than her father.

Remember that we called puberty "the chum stage." The young girl takes to herself a bosom companion of the same sex with whom she shares her "secrets." One of the chief dangers to arise during this part of the growing-up process comes from this relationship, which is, of course, a normal one under optimum circumstances. However, if the chum selected turns out to be precocious as far as sexual experiment with the opposite sex is concerned, the friendship can lead to harmful experiences for the more innocent member of the duo.

A girl entering puberty is often attracted to a girl a year or two older than she is and will idealize this new friend, feeling that any action she performs is entirely fine and defensible. Neither of these children is, of course, ready for any truly heterosexual experience, but the younger one may imitate the older one and attempt to follow through in a sexual relationship with a boy or older man. Without mentioning the possible disaster of pregnancy at this early juncture, I should like to emphasize that sexual intercourse at this age, without the preparatory stage of adolescence having intervened, can cause a permanent aversion for the experience. It can produce a trauma of such severity that the young person may withdraw from the opposite sex entirely and remain withdrawn. Or it may encourage her to believe that she has attained her majority and cause her to act out this joyless and premature experience over and over with many different members of the opposite sex.

The simple fact is that a girl is not ready for love-making until she falls in love with a specific individual. For this to happen in a meaningful manner, she must first pass through the daydream stage of adolescence. Boys do not go through this phase and, indeed, do not have to. They are ready for intercourse at a much younger age than girls are. Girls have much to risk in love, even if we confine our observations to the purely biological aspects of the experience of sexual intercourse. Psychologically they must, so to speak, be sure that it is indeed Prince Charming who leans over them. Until it is, they must dream and sleep, for if it is a rude stranger he can shatter the dream forever, thus rob the young girl of any chance of ever bringing her dream to fulfillment in reality.

Another danger of both puberty and adolescence is that the parents will be overly strict, interpreting the move of the young one toward independence as a danger to her. I have seen many cases of young girls who might have stayed within the home until their adolescence was safely over had it not been for the rather prurient and thick-skinned assumption of a mother or father, or both, that their early dating must inevitably be immoral. This assumption on the part of a parent can activate a very hostile reaction on the part of a young girl. It is as if the parent were saying to her, "You will never be independent of us, never have a life of your own. Why don't you give up trying?" The fact that the parents do not intend their watchfulness to imply this at all is not relevant. That's the way the young one too often interprets it, and in a gesture of defiance she may do something that will really injure her.

Equally seriously affected, if not more so, is the young girl who *feels* extremely rebellious but who submits to overzealous parental authority out of fear. I have seen several girls with this problem. What generally happens is that they have pulled back, because of undue parental influences, from indulging the personality-enriching dreams of adolescence. This causes them to remain on the threshold of womanhood, lost in an emotional dependency which belongs to an earlier phase of development. By and large, the problems of such girls when they come to womanhood tend to be more severe than those of the girls who rebelled.

In making these observations on parental strictness I am in no way advocating a laissez-faire attitude. Every young girl needs to feel the force of the parents' moral feelings; they give her guidance and a feeling of security. She will, however, generally react more normally and healthfully if the moral attitudes are expressed and interpreted rather than laid down as ukases.

We have now seen the stages of development that lead to maturity in woman and the pitfalls she may encounter on the way. With this final information in hand we are at last ready to look at frigidity itself. The next section, therefore, will treat of the frigid woman herself, and I will show you, with specific cases, how the kinds and degrees of frigidity develop and what concrete problems they bring in their train. With such models in mind we will then be prepared to examine the constructive steps which individuals who suffer from this problem must take to win their freedom, to cross the bridge to womanhood.

SECTION *III*   *The Fear of Love—*
Case Histories

Chapter 10

TOTAL AND PARTIAL FRIGIDITY

Although we have discussed the various types of frigidity in a former chapter, I think it will be helpful now to go into the matter in greater detail. I am going to illustrate the major types of frigidity with case histories. In this way you can get a living picture of each problem.

I think the case method of presentation is particularly helpful to a full grasp of frigidity. Those who are caught up in the problem usually lose their objectivity about themselves, are unable to see with any real clarity just how their actions and reactions are neurotic and just how they are affecting those about them. The true story of another woman who has suffered from the same affliction mirrors the problem faithfully, allows one to achieve a clear view of herself, perhaps for the first time. For the fact is that each kind of frigidity has its own very distinctive characteristics and its own unique causes.

But as you read these cases I think you will be struck by the very special differences in each kind of frigidity, which will allow you to see your own image—to diagnose yourself, so to speak. You will see, too, that there are certain characteristics common to all the frigidities. Knowledge of both these facts, as you will discover, is important to the cure of the frigid woman.

In giving these stories I cannot, of course, include examples of all the pitfalls that are encountered from childhood to adulthood. That would require much more space than I have here. I will attempt, rather, to select cases of frigidity caused by experiences most common to our society.

The first case, then, is one of total frigidity. This kind, as you may recall from our earlier description of it, is one of the most severe forms of sexual disorder in women and is widely prevalent. Without further ado I give you the case of a woman we shall call Patricia Agnew.

When Patricia Agnew came to my office for her first interview, she had not come, consciously, to consult me for a frigidity problem or to discuss the results of such a problem on her marriage. She came because she was having, in her words, "another nervous breakdown."

She was not a very good-looking woman, though she had nice teeth and large blue eyes. It was her figure that was striking. In direct contrast to her inner attitude, her figure was round and voluptuous, almost the American ideal of what is considered "sexy." Her lips were full and sensual, but she held them tightly together, which gave her a censorious, critical, old-maidish look. She was thirty-six years old.

Her "nervous breakdowns" (she persisted in using the expression, though it was clearly inapplicable in her case), she told me, were recurrent. She had had them for three successive years. Each of them had started with a very marked increase in inner tension. She would feel growingly unable to cope with the manifold social and familial demands of her life; a great sense of inadequacy would set in gradually and she would become listless and depressed. Finally the slightest task would seem too much and she would now start to have day-long bouts of weeping. During such periods she suffered from chronic insomnia, and when she was able to snatch a few hours of sleep she would often have repetitive, nightmarish dreams in which she was pursued by criminals.

At the beginning of our talks Patricia would become extremely guarded whenever I attempted to open any discussion of a personal nature. She had come for help with the express conviction that I, the doctor, should find a quick and easy solution to her periods of acute anxiety: drugs, a sea voyage, anything that did not entail looking inward, taking responsibility for her condition. This evasiveness, this desire to find easy solutions, is characteristic of all forms of frigidity in women, but it is sometimes extremely pronounced in the type of frigidity this patient suffered from.

However, as Patricia developed confidence and trust in me, the real facts gradually emerged. She had been married for ten years and had two children, six and eight. Her husband was socially prominent, financially successful, and (as I saw for myself later, when I had a few discussions with him) strikingly handsome, a slender, tall, dark-haired man with a gentle and charming manner.

During her entire marriage this patient had never had, she finally told me, "one solid hour of happiness." From the very beginning she had quarreled with her husband, and the domestic strife, at least on her part, had become truly bitter after the birth of their first son. She had felt that her husband was becoming increasingly cruel, selfish, demanding, and insensitive to her needs. She had believed that he was trying to impose his will on her in any and all situations and that it was an absolute necessity to struggle against this domination. "I felt as if he would shatter my integrity if I didn't put up a fight," she told me. "It was as though he wished to have me as a slave, nothing less; it was either he or I."

The quarrels were generally over the most trifling matters, and though her husband almost invariably tried to make up within a few hours, she would rebuff him, and consequently bitter feelings would often endure for a week or more at a time. These battles of will, or power struggles, would terminate only, it became evident, when she had felt that he had been sufficiently punished for his transgressions, though she confessed that by the time she was ready to forgive him she had often forgotten what the original quarrel had been all about.

She felt, too (still felt and always had), that her husband was extremely critical of her and that he never really gave her full approval for anything. She believed that he did not like the way she dressed, the way she conducted herself socially, or the way she managed the children. When I asked her just how he expressed his disapproval of her, to give me an example, she could not think of anything specific and concluded lamely: "Well, he usually praises me to my face, but I can tell by his expression that he doesn't mean it."

Later, in the areas she had specifically mentioned, I checked with her husband on his attitudes. He told me that he had felt at the beginning and still felt that his wife dressed beautifully and that she was absolutely perfect at any kind of social function. "She has a really remarkable gift for conversation of any kind with practically any person," he said. On the other hand, he had sometimes felt that she tended to be too permissive with the children and that she worried about them excessively. However, he had learned early that he could not help her in this matter and only prayed that the children would have no adverse effects from her tendency to pamper them. I should like to report that, as she recovered, Patricia gradually became aware of the fact that this "critical" attitude she had ascribed to her husband was almost entirely a product of her personal problem.

Another powerful conviction she possessed was that her husband did not really love her. She felt that he was mainly interested in exploiting her, both for his "selfish" sexual needs and to advance his business. At the beginning of their marriage her husband had entered his father's engineering firm and at once had been faced with the necessity of doing a great deal of entertaining. His wife, he soon found out, was an excellent hostess and he came to depend on her gracious parties mightily. His dependency on her collaboration she at once took for exploitation and even extended that to mean: "He doesn't love me; he merely finds me a convenience. Any other presentable woman would suit him as well." There was another twist to this irrational conviction, though it was more hidden and did not emerge until quite late in the treatment. Her feelings might be expressed in these words: "He didn't succeed on his own; I made him what he is, even if I never get the credit for it." Imagine, with an underlying feeling of this kind, how much chance for survival any tender feelings toward her husband might have.

As the sessions continued and Mrs. Agnew gained more and more confidence, she began to feel freer about discussing her sexual life. She at length confessed that she had never experienced any sexual pleasure in her entire life, neither before nor after her marriage. At no point, could she recall, had she ever masturbated or attempted to do so, even in early childhood. Kissing or being stroked gave her no sensations whatsoever. From the beginning, intercourse had been distasteful and often painful, though sometimes she took a slight satisfaction from the obvious pleasure her husband obtained from orgasm.

The actual sexual life of this couple had been at a virtual standstill for nearly eight years. Intercourse occurred, at most, at three-month intervals. It was never spontaneous. The husband was required to make an appointment for a "date" several days before actual intercourse. His wife would acquiesce to such a tryst only after she had refused him several times and had accumulated a great deal of guilt for so doing.

From the moment she made the appointment she would become anxious, and this would increase to the point where she was filled with actual dread. Often she would be forced to break the appointment and postpone it. As the time for the intercourse approached she would also experience feelings of rage, repeat to herself over and over, "Why *must* I, why *must* I?" In preparing for the act itself (putting her diaphragm in, inserting the jelly), she would linger for as much as an hour while her husband waited. She often found that her vaginal muscles contracted to such a degree that the insertion of the diaphragm was painful and difficult to accomplish.

With her misery increasing momently, she went, after these preparations, to the marital bed as one might to the executioner. Her husband's looks repelled her now; his nakedness seemed disgusting and offensive. She saw him as "skinny, white, and ugly, with an enormous penis. It was as if he were nothing but a big disgusting sexual organ."

It goes without saying that she could feel no tenderness or warmth—she could not even simulate it. She remained totally passive throughout the entire act, which her husband, in response to her rejection (as she later, in happier times, learned), hurried through as quickly as possible. It is interesting to note that, despite her own inability to respond, one of her bitterest complaints about her husband was that his love-making was mechanical, hasty, and that he never showed any tenderness.

It had never occurred to her, of course, that he might be reacting to her clear aversion to the whole process. Indeed, she saw no justification for his shamefaced approach to her until she was well on the road to sexual health. It is usual in such cases for the wife to blame the husband for her failures, no matter how glaringly unreasonable and untrue her accusation may be.

After intercourse she was always depressed. She felt "dirty and used." Her husband's semen appeared to her to be disgusting. "All I wanted was to get to sleep fast and to forget the whole episode until the next ordeal became necessary," she said.

Under such circumstances it is difficult to understand how a marriage could exist at all. However, such marriages do exist in great numbers, and by far the majority of them do not end up in the divorce courts, as one might expect. Despite the bitter complainings, the struggle for power, the fear of love, and the dread of sex on the wife's part, I have found that there is usually a well-hidden but genuine bond of love between the couple. The husband seems originally to have seen in his now quarrelsome partner a part that can be truly loving, truly warm. It may show dimly and only in the interstices of the relationship, but it keeps hope alive in him that she will come into her true self one day; he warms himself as best he can, meanwhile, at her meager fires.

But now that we have seen a picture of the totally frigid woman let us examine the causes for it. I have stated that every kind of frigidity has its special cause. What was the cause in Patricia Agnew's case?

To understand the origins of her problem, we will have to explore her earliest history, particularly her relationship to her mother and father. She was an only child, and her father was clearly the dominant figure in the household. He was an extremely successful and lovable man. He abounded in all the virtues, was infinitely patient and loving with his little daughter. She told me that from her earliest times she considered him, physically speaking, "an enormously beautiful man," and in describing him she lingered lovingly over the details of his appearance—his "sculptured head," "wonderful deep kindly eyes," "marvelously athletic figure." A psychiatrist, of course, would pay very close attention to such an ecstatic description, coming as it did from such an otherwise withdrawn person.

By way of contrast she had considered her mother "mousy" and, while she had liked her in a general sense, she had never consciously had any very strong positive feelings about her.

Patricia clearly had been a "daddy's girl." There is nothing wrong, of course, with this under normal circumstances; had she grown up to be sexually free and had she been able to transfer her early love feelings from her father to other men, this early attachment to the father would have been merely a phase in normal development.

It is not necessary here to depict the stages by which Patricia and I arrived at a clear understanding of the early problem that had caused her later frigidity. It will be enough to state the events themselves.

You will recall the fact that in the first five years of life the child is a very sensual little being. Patricia had been no exception in the beginning; she had transferred these feelings, in the normal course of events, to her father. However, this powerful and charming man whose personality dominated the household, overshadowing his wife completely, had been far too responsive (unwittingly, of course) to the little girl's erotic feelings. He dandled her and played with her endlessly, surrounded her with a stimulating warmth, psychologically and physically; he showered kisses and hugs, compliments and candy upon her; he gave her anything and everything to express his devotion to her.

The consequence? The very strength of his love, its varied and aggressive forms, its unrelenting intensity, had a negative effect on the child. To put it most simply, his love overstimulated her budding sexuality. This powerful man's love overwhelmed her. Her small ego could not handle such powerful feelings; they frightened her. In order to cope with such feelings, therefore, she had had to repress them powerfully, deny their existence.

Children can do this, as you will remember from our discussion of the latency period of childhood. It is at the onset of this period, which occurs at about six years of age, that infantile sexuality is pushed under ground, to remain dormant until puberty. Patricia, under the influence of her prematurely strong sexual response to her father, had been forced to enter her latency period, we were able to determine, at the far too early age of four.

With sex out of the way, she was now able to indulge her worship of her father in complete "innocence." He was a man who believed passionately in success, and his ebullience, love of life, and high intelligence had won him a great deal of it. His young daughter felt now that to win his love she must achieve and achieve, endlessly. From the first grade of school through her last year at college, therefore, she bent all her efforts to excelling mentally. But her father was also a perfectionist; he expected top honors from himself and jeered at anything less in himself. Thoughtlessly he made the same demands on his daughter. Since she did not have his qualifications she was not always able to come up to his standards in every field of endeavor; few could have equaled his demands. When she did not achieve such top honors she felt that she was not worthy of her father's love and indeed that he did not love her. He did nothing to correct this feeling.

If you will recall our normal stages of development for the growing child, you will easily see that when marriage time came around Patricia Agnew had not touched first, second, or third base. She had appeared to be growing normally, excelling in schoolwork, playing the role of the dutiful daughter, going out on dates. But in the emotional and sexual spheres she had been arrested at a very early stage.

So severe had been her repression of her childhood sexuality that when the glandular changes which usher in puberty occurred she failed to have the resurgence of sexual feeling and the development of psychological characteristics normal for that period. For that reason she omitted her adolescent phase of development, too, the period of young love's long and lovely dream which prepares the girl for the activities of love sexually and psychologically. How could she have had such a dream? It depends on the development of a true and normal sexuality. The door had been locked on her sexuality in infancy and the key thrown away.

Psychologically, too, she was an infant. The need to excel, to master one's environment, is of course normal for the latency period. Nature has arranged this period, sagely put sex out of the way for a few years so that the ego may have a chance to grow, to prepare itself for the sexual storms and stresses of puberty and adolescence.

However, since in a very real sense she could not pass through puberty and adolescence, she had remained psychologically in the latency period, the non-sexual, competitive, father-worshiping childhood period.

Patricia really had two distinct attitudes toward her husband. The first was expressed in her quarrelsomeness, her belief that he was selfish, unattractive, and unlovable. This attitude was based on the fact that, very literally, her heart still belonged to Daddy. With her exaggerated childhood feelings toward her father, every other man suffered by comparison, seemed unworthy of her love. Her husband was an interloper who came between her and her ideal. Therefore, his normal need for her to love him, to be a good wife to him, seemed hateful to her, filled her with rage. Sex under such circumstances was a virtual rape of Lucrece, with the husband playing the role of the dark and frightening rapist, the father representing her true love, for whom she must preserve her innocence and purity.

Another deeper and more hidden attitude was the exact opposite of this, indeed contradictory to it. In this aspect of her mind her husband stood for her father. Thus sexual feelings toward such a person must be entirely taboo; she must repress them as she had in her earliest years and she must keep them repressed. Too, she must excel in all the things her father wanted her to excel in. To her husband she must primarily excel in her wifely functions, and this was the essential trap. For because she very consciously knew she was not and under the circumstances could not be even a passable wife, she was constantly inundated by feelings of inadequacy and inferiority.

You can see then what a complete trap Patricia was in.

Actually, unless she had been strongly motivated to seek help, she would never have found an exit from her difficulties. Her periodic "breakdowns" were a simple and direct expression of the hopelessness of her situation. It was as if she were saying: "I am truly a helpless child; I can do nothing grown-up. I must be taken care of as a child is."

She did recover her lost sexuality and her lost capacity for happiness, and in a later chapter we shall see how the Patricia Agnews of this life can achieve such an outcome. But before we leave her I should like to make one further observation of a general kind: Consider how totally beyond any help she would have been if her irrational opposition to her husband, to sex, and to real love between the sexes had been bolstered up, made to seem quite justifiable by a philosophy of life based on the feminist school of thought. From such a standpoint every one of her difficulties would have been considered perfectly normal!

Patricia, of course, represents frigidity in its most extreme form, the type in which there is almost a total lack of sexual feeling. To clarify this subject, recall our frigidity scale. On this scale total frigidity would needle around zero. A woman at the opposite end of this scale would experience a great deal of sexual excitement before and during intercourse but would be unable to have orgasm, or her orgasm would be so weak and unsatisfying that it would leave her very consciously unsatisfied. (Normalcy, of course, is a more or less absolute state and could not be described in terms of degrees.) We rate her near or at 100 on the frigidity scale, meaning she is close to normalcy. In between these two extremes there is every possible degree of sexual blocking.

Women who suffer from some degree of frigidity (rather than from a type of frigidity, such as our "masculine type") have personality problems similar to Patricia's. These problems become milder as they go up the scale toward normalcy. The underlying structure of their problem is also similar to Patricia's—it is based on a too strong and too early attachment to their fathers. This early attachment has survived into adulthood and, depending largely on its original strength, causes a greater or lesser degree of sexual and interpersonal problems in marriage.

But as we go up the scale toward greater sexual responsiveness the difference in degree seems almost to become a difference in kind. From roughly the middle of the scale upward, the essential sexual problem has little to do with withdrawnness or unbridled or unrelenting hostility toward one's mate, or a feeling of being exploited sexually. It is far more closely connected with direct sexual frustration, with a kind of Tantalus-like feeling that one is terribly close to one's goal but cannot quite achieve it.

Here is an example of what I mean. I shall call this patient Joan. She was twenty-eight years old when she came to me, a pretty woman with an upturned nose, a generally insouciant manner, and a pleased-with-life smile. She had been married two years, she told me, and came directly to her problem. During intercourse she would become tremendously excited most of the time. It took little to stimulate her, and as the intercourse continued she would maintain her high level of excitement. But on most occasions, no matter how long the love-making continued, she would reach no climax at all. She was left with a frustrated, almost frantic feeling.

There were, however, occasional exceptions to this rule. In about one out of ten times Joan would achieve a climax of sorts during love-making. But it was weak and inconclusive and not by any means deeply satisfying to her, as it should have been and as she felt it could be. Here, however, is the most important point. Whenever she did experience this climax she almost invariably woke the next morning with severe back pains which lasted for two or three days and were clearly psychosomatic. And she would feel irritable and anxious. It was *only* on such days that she experienced personal difficulties with her husband. She would find herself arguing with him about trifles, being generally crossgrained and countersuggestible.

"I should think," she said to me in puzzlement, "that it would be just the other way around; that I would be difficult with him when I didn't come to any climax and pleased and hopeful when I did, even if it wasn't the perfect orgasm."

But Joan was being merely logical in this assumption. The mind is not necessarily run by such rational considerations. When she was able to comprehend the reasons behind the apparent anomaly of her backaches and her anxiety reactions, she was close to being cured.

Joan's problem was a truly mild one. Her relationship with her husband was basically as sound as a dollar; she thought him attractive physically and respected him. She enjoyed their social life together and never felt exploited or put upon when he had to entertain his business associates. Indeed, she had a great deal of fun playing the role of hostess to them. There was no area where one could find real difficulty between Joan and her husband except in their sexual life.

This problem washed out very quickly, for it was lightly held in the soil of Joan's personality. And yet in exploring it we found it had exactly the same structure as Patricia Agnew's problem: a basic overattachment to her father that had occurred in early childhood and had not been resolved. The difference was that the attachment on Joan's part had been a much milder one than Patricia's had been, and therefore, while it did have a lingering aftereffect, it did not encompass Joan's entire personality and was therefore far easier to deal with.

There were two things that made Joan's relationship with her father less destructive than Patricia's had been. First, Joan's father was not *so* overpoweringly loving and attentive to the little girl during the first six years of her growth. Second, Joan's mother had a very distinctive and strong personality of her own, and Joan had had a good relationship with her all during her formative years. This neutralized to a certain extent the overstimulating effect of her father. It had allowed her to identify with her own sex in a healthy manner, to give her the feeling that it was a fine thing to be a sweetheart, wife, and mother.

Joan's frigidity problem was helped in a few sessions. One day she came to me and was very upset. Her last intercourse had been successful and had culminated in the strongest orgasm she had had up to this time. But, as usual, the next day had been an anxious one and she had had a severe backache.

As she talked about it she suddenly said: "I had the most amazing dream; I've just recalled it." She had been on a swing in a playground, she told me, and her father had been pushing her. "I flew higher and higher," she said. "It was like flying. The sensations were delicious. I hoped he would never stop. Then suddenly I looked around and he had turned into some kind of criminal or something. He seized me and I screamed, but somehow I knew nobody could hear me. I then suddenly remembered something a girl friend had actually told me in college when a group of us were discussing rape. She had said that a woman might be killed if she resisted. And she said that if it ever happened to her she would just relax and try to enjoy it. I recalled this now, and the criminal in my dream did rape me and I enjoyed it thoroughly. I came to a terrific climax, a kind I've never had in real life."

She had awakened at this point but then went back to

sleep and had the following nightmare. "Women policemen were pursuing me for having committed some crime," she said. "They'd almost catch me, but I'd get away. Finally one of them did catch me, but when I looked in her face she was smiling at me tenderly and she said: 'Don't worry; it's not so terrible after all.' "

Knowing what you know already, it should not be too hard to see what Joan's dream means. The swinging, with her father doing the pushing, represented her very early sexual feelings toward her father. When these became too direct she disguised them by turning her father into the criminal rapist. Actually *she* was the one who felt like the criminal, and it is borne out by the fact that in the following dream she was pursued by the police. It is significant that they were policewomen, for the little girl feels very strong guilt toward her mother because of the forbidden and taboo sex feelings toward her father. The forgiving attitude of the policewoman represented both her good relationship with her mother and her inner readiness to get over the problem.

There could scarcely be a better illustration of the whole theory of modern psychoanalysis than this. To Joan, at least, it was eminently clear. Her terror, expressed by her dream of the pursuing policewomen, disappeared before that session was over, and she stood ready to move into a mature and satisfying sexuality with her husband. With her conscious mind she now knew that she had been frightened of complete sexual love because, in the highest reaches of passion, her feelings for her husband unconsciously reminded her of the "dangerous" feelings she had once felt for her father; thus she dared not indulge them to the utmost. Understanding the irrational basis of her fears allowed her to dispense with them.

Chapter 11

THE MASCULINE WOMAN

She was a strikingly handsome woman. I looked at her as she sat opposite me in my office and I remember being struck by the extreme femininity of her appearance: the glossy, clean softness of her brown hair, the peaches-and-cream texture of her complexion, the care she had given her toilette and her clothes. Everything was perfect. I recall I thought then: "Perhaps a little too perfect. It's almost as if she is dressing for a role."

First impressions are not always correct, but in this case mine were. My new patient, whom I shall call Toni (her real nickname was also based on a boy's name) was suffering from the form of frigidity that is often called the "masculinity complex." She was, in short, the "clitoridal woman," whose general characteristics we looked at briefly before. Her case is so typical and illustrates so many aspects of this very widespread type of frigidity that I have selected it to tell here.

In my first sessions with her I could see that Toni's clear thinking and logical mind, her emotionless, almost masculine forthrightness in expressing herself belied her softly feminine appearance. Her way of dressing was an unconscious attempt to hide from the world, and from herself, her real problem.

She was thirty years old, had been married for seven years, and had a five-year-old son. For the past two years she had had severe migraine headaches, sometimes as often

as three times a week. These headaches had started at about
the same time that serious marriage difficulties had developed between herself and her husband. The problem, she
stated honestly, had originated with her. Rather quickly she
seemed to have lost all respect for her husband. Looking
at him one day, she said, she suddenly saw that he had no
ambition of any kind and was "insufferably smug and complacent." He had not the slightest desire to better his lot,
she realized, but was content to putter around in his cellar
workshop with "inane and useless projects" or to spend his
evenings "glued to the television set" or playing poker with
a few "useless men."

This passivity on the part of her husband had inexplica-
bly enraged her. "I realized in that moment that we could
rot, socially and financially, if it were up to him," she told
me bitterly. "I can't stand such pointlessness in a man."

I now asked her what their social life together had been
like, and she told me that it had been very active until two
years before. "Most of our friends were my friends originally. His friends just seemed to fall away in the first year
of our marriage. They weren't very interesting anyhow, and
I was just as glad. But after I began to lose interest in
my husband, to lose my respect for him, I began to withdraw socially myself. My husband didn't seem to care
about that either. He doesn't seem to care about anything."

Further inquiry elicited the fact that Toni was extremely
successful in the business world. She had been through a
leading woman's college and had been the president of her
class and very prominent in extracurricular activities. "I was
a really Big Woman On Campus," she said nostalgically. She
had then gone to graduate school, taking her degree at
Columbia University in business administration, and on graduation had entered the buying department of one of the
largest merchandising corporations in America.

Within five years Toni had become the top buyer of
women's clothes for the entire corporation. In actuality this
was one of the top positions of this kind in the United
States, for the merchandising corporation was gigantic. Her
present salary exceeded twenty-five thousand dollars a year.

I was not surprised to learn, at this point, that this was
exactly three times the salary her husband made as a junior
member of a law firm that specialized in corporation law.

I now asked Toni if she did not get a great deal of
pleasure from her success in the business world. She told
me that before she was married and for about two years
afterward she had indeed felt a great deal of pride in her

success. Her husband, too, had shared her pleasure in her achievements. After the baby had come, however, he had seemed gradually to lose interest in her work. And gradually, too, she had developed a growing sense of guilt about her activities in the business world. She had the constant feeling that she was neglecting her child. Sometimes she would call the nurse at home five or six times a day to find out if the baby was all right. "Two months ago," she told me, "I went in to see my boss. I told him I wanted to leave or to cut down to a part-time job. He was terribly upset and at once offered me a large increase and gave me a big talk on how important I was and how much they needed me. One part of me was flattered enormously, but after I left him I felt depressed. I felt as though I were failing my child terribly, but I felt trapped by the amount of money I had been offered. I also felt that if I should really give it all up I would quickly become bored at just staying home."

Everything Toni had said up to this point fitted the classical picture of the clitoridal woman. Almost invariably they marry a passive and rather dependent (though often very attractive and charming) man and finally become bitterly critical of his dependency and lack of drive, thus upsetting the equilibrium of the marriage. In their mind's eye they wish for a more aggressive male who would dominate them, but this is pure fantasy, for they would not be able to stand real male assertiveness and, indeed, take it very poorly when their passive male does assert himself. Such women, too, are often very successful in the world of masculine achievement. And if they have children they develop great guilt about neglecting them.

One further characteristic that Toni had was a tremendous anxiety about childbirth. Her pregnancy had been characterized by a very deep depression; she had suffered physically for the entire nine months and, when the time for delivery arrived, had felt "absolutely certain that I was going to die."

Knowing all this, a psychiatrist could almost guess the nature of Toni's sexual life. It did not come out in our interviews for some time, and I did not press for the details. However, when the facts did emerge at length they portrayed the particular type of sexual response which characterizes the clitoridal woman and has caused endless and ill-informed speculation in various quarters. The fact that this form of frigidity is so widespread in our society has actually given rise to a group which believes that the clitoridal woman's form of sexual gratification is perfectly normal. This group is vociferous and much-published and, in my opinion at least, can do incalculable harm if its conclusions should reach wide acceptance.

Toni was what we call "clitorally centered," though she did have some general reactions to kissing and other forms of foreplay. For example, she enjoyed having her back rubbed and she received a rather minor pleasure if her husband manipulated her labia. But she definitely preferred that the foreplay be confined to her clitoris. If her husband stroked her labia for more than a few seconds, the sensations became rather uncomfortable and she would ask him to stop.

Orgasm was almost invariably confined to the clitoris. During such orgasm, though her vagina sometimes became lubricated, she felt no pleasurable sensations there at all. At the point of orgasm she could feel no vaginal contractions nor any desire to have her husband thrust his penis ever deeper or more rapidly inside her, as is chracteristic of the normal orgasm in women.

On the contrary, she generally preferred to be masturbated manually rather than to have sexual intercourse. Often, to avoid intercourse, she would masturbate her husband. Or, when they did have sexual intercourse, her husband would generally masturbate Toni afterward.

However, she was occasionally able to have a clitoral orgasm during intercourse. This always was achieved when she took the position on top and her husband was on the bottom. She was very circumstantial in her explanation of why she could achieve orgasm in this position, pointing out to me at some length that her clitoris could come into more direct contact with his penis in this position. There may be some truth in this fact, but what was of more interest to me was the extent to which she went to make her point clear. I have often found that women with this type of problem are, in the beginning at any rate, very anxious to avoid any suggestion that they may be enjoying the position because in our society it is the traditional male position in intercourse.

Just as she took the lead in financial and social matters in the family so did Toni take the lead in sexual matters. It was she who almost invariably initiated every intercourse. She explained this fact to me by saying that her husband was very insensitive to her sensual moods. "He just doesn't seem to pick up any cues that I throw out," she said, "so I have to go after him when I feel passionate." Please note that this, too, is a reversal of the usual pattern in sexual love between men and women in our society; the woman will sometimes initiate sex, but it is usually the man who does so.

It is interesting, too, to note that although the personal relationship between Toni and her husband had deteriorated badly in the two years before she came to me there had been no diminution in the amount of sex they had. Since Toni was the initiator of sex, the one who, so to speak, set the sexual pace of the relationship, it would indicate that she had split off her sexual feelings from other emotions. Unlike most women, she could have sex with a person toward whom, at least during this period, she felt no conscious feelings of love.

As soon as I possibly could, without upsetting her, I began to focus my discussions with Toni on the period two years before, when she began to develop feelings of anger toward her husband.

At first our discussions yielded nothing, though I had emphasized to Toni the importance of reconstructing all the details of life at that juncture as minutely as possible. At length she brought up the important factor. Two days before the sudden onset of her intensely critical feelings toward her husband she had, for the first time in her life, pleasurable vaginal sensations during intercourse.

She had felt very warmly toward her husband that night; an unaccustomed tenderness had filled her whole being before the love-making. They had had no preliminary love play of the usual manual kind, starting intercourse almost at once. The vaginal sensations had begun halfway through the intercourse and had been maintained right up to the point of orgasm, when her clitoral sensations once more took over. She recalled that afterward she had been surprised and quite pleased but had soon "forgotten" the whole experience.

There could be no doubt that Toni's anger at her husband and her migraines started right after this sexual experience. And there could be no doubt that they were intimately related experiences. Though her personality structure and the psychological events which caused her kind of frigidity were different from Patricia's and from Joan's, they were alike in one regard. All three had the deepest and most abiding fear of real vaginal sensation and ultimately, of course, of vaginal orgasm.

This fear is a profound one in the clitoridal or masculine woman. Toni, rather than admit to herself how frightened she was of this vaginal experience, chose unconsciously to ruin her personal relationship with her husband, to denigrate all those characteristics which she had formerly loved in him—his charm, his ability to relax, his quiet and warm understanding, his refusal to be driven by circumstances, and his insistence on enjoying the small, warm, everyday events of life. To protect herself from knowing the real nature of her problem, she had to blame him for her difficulties. She even had to make up the difficulties, for though he was a rather passive man he was also a very attractive and loving one.

The vagina is the very center of femininity, of female love, as we have seen. If the individual fears this love, she learns unconsciously to block vaginal sensations. If, however, at any point in her life she is beguiled into feeling sensation there, she will have a severe anxiety reaction, flee from the experience in any way she can. And this brings us to the psychological structure of this kind of problem.

The clitoridal woman develops, very early, an underlying denial that she is indeed feminine or that she has any use for the things of womanhood. She learns to feel that womanhood is dangerous, a slavish and humiliating role. Only men are powerful and secure; and thus she identifies herself with the male exclusively.

If you will recall that, sexual anatomy aside, there is little to distinguish boys from girls either psychologically or glandularly in the first ten years of existence, you will get some indication that the desire to be a boy need not seem so impossible of fulfillment to a little girl. And even if we take her sexual anatomy into consideration, the idea does not seem farfetched to her. She does have a clitoris, which, in her wishful psychology, she can consider a penis, or at least the beginnings of one. Though it is small it is, in medical parlance, "the homologue of the penis." It can become erect; it has a head; it has a prepuce. Girls who are going to pursue (albeit unconsciously) their daydreams of becoming male, eschewing femininity, pay a great deal of very minute attention to these similarities.

Such was the case with Toni. Typically for such cases, her father had rejected her. During the stage of development when a young daughter needs a sufficient quota of her father's love and tenderness to give her an experience of the rewards of womanhood, a substrate of feminine security, he simply ignored her. He was, by all accounts, a very cold man, engrossed in his business and quite indifferent to both his wife and daughter. The concept that men rejected women, were actively hostile to them, was very much deepened in Toni by the fact that her father behaved in exactly an opposite manner to her brother, who was three years younger. This young fellow received, by all accounts, the lion's share of her father's small store of attention and devotion.

Reports from a patient, while they have a certain reliability, cannot always be depended on completely. In Toni's case I was fortunate to be able to check the veracity of her story. She had maintained a close relationship with her brother after they had grown up and, on Toni's insistence, I saw him. If anything, Toni had understated the degree of her father's withdrawn relationship to her and her mother.

Even at that, the damage to Toni's ability to love might not have been decisive had her mother been a warm and feminine woman. But here, too, circumstances militated against the little girl. Her mother (perhaps as a reaction against her husband's personality but more likely because she, too, was essentially a masculinized woman) refused to stay home with the children after her son had achieved the age of three. She had opened a dress shop with a friend in the business section of Toni's home town which had been very successful, demanding all her time. It was a rare evening when Toni's mother got home for dinner. Between the ages of seven and fourteen the girl saw her mother little more than an hour a day on weekdays and half a day on Sundays.

It is not hard to see then that Toni's young world had little in it that supported feminine values. It was clear to her that only male activities, achievement in terms of male goals, could bring security. Even her mother seemed to subscribe to this, for hadn't she gone back into the world of male activity as soon as she could manage it? Indeed, judging the matter by her father's relationship to her brother, she very early reached the literal conclusion that in order to achieve love a woman really had to *be* a man.

If we were to examine the purely sexual side of Toni's unconscious identification with the male sex, we would only have to examine the dreams she brought to our sessions. At the beginning she would frequently have dreams in which she was dressed as a man or in which she was excelling in male sports. I have recorded one incredible dream, really quite a funny one in a sense were it not so basically pathetic, in which she played quarterback for Harvard in the annual Yale-Harvard football game. In my notes taken at the time I wrote that she made four touch-downs!

In her conscious mind Toni could not recall whether in her childhood she actually believed she might turn into a boy. More disturbed women than she often do remember such conscious fantasies in girlhood. However, on a deeper level there is little doubt that Toni treasured the possibility of such a metamorphosis. As time wore on, of course, reality and her own good intelligence modified and disguised her wish. She repressed the desire to be a boy in a physically external way, by growing a literal penis. And she substituted for this concrete idea fantasies of achievement in, to her, the male sense. In high school and college she threw herself into a world of intellectual and extracurricular activity and made an astonishing, almost legendary, record for herself. In the college she attended she became not only the president of her class but the editor of the school newspaper and president of the college's century-old literary society.

Sexually Toni did not abandon clitoral masturbation in adolescence as, under normal circumstances, a girl would, or at least would attempt to. She clung to this early form of sexual release with almost grim determination, masturbating daily at least once. This continuation of clitoral masturbation long after the time when it is normally given up was, of course, the sexual sequel to her early rejection of all that was feminine.

At this point one might be willing to grant that Toni had sufficient reason to embrace masculine values but wonder just why she should develop such a strong rejection of her feminine side, such a fear of it. The question becomes more urgent when we learn that Toni's sex instruction was handled in an apparently intelligent manner by her mother. Sex, menstruation, pregnancy, and other related matters were explained to her calmly and clearly and at just the right times to satisfy her normal curiosity.

She had no shocking experience, nobody seduced her; nothing whatsoever that was visibly untoward had happened to her.

Many girls can be turned against sexuality by experiences that are directly traumatic. Such experiences, however, are not an absolute prerequisite for later difficulties. If you will recall our earlier discussion, you will remember that to embrace the feminine role a woman must be willing in the deepest biological and psychological sense to suspend the natural law of self-preservation. She must be willing to sacrifice her time, her being, her other goals—her very life—to give birth to her children and to see them safely to maturity.

If in her formative years the young girl is not properly prepared for this role, if womanhood is not treated as desirable, honorable, and lovable, she will automatically turn against it. The game, to the young mind, will seem far too risky for the candle. As the years pass, nothing disproves this contention and the original childlike fears, unmodified by reality, remain intact or even increase.

In other words, to the improperly prepared child, facing the reality of being a woman is in itself traumatic. Such was the case with Toni. She was convinced that real love, full of giving and willing sacrifice, represented death. It is no wonder then that two years before she saw me, when she had come to the verge of experiencing something like true sexual pleasure with her husband, she turned against it in a panic, barred it from her consciousness, attempted to render unlovable the man who had dared to rouse such dangerous feelings in her.

In telling of Toni's story I have selected a rather pure type of clitoridal woman, but I should like to make clear that not all cases show such an obvious masculinization. Nor am I making the point that the woman who succeeds in the market place is necessarily dominated by masculine motives. A woman can be a stay-at-home, apparently performing all her duties as a wife and mother, and still be suffering from the same kind of basic problem that confronted Toni. Perhaps we can put it this way: many women of this kind have never learned to imitate men as successfully as Toni did.

Helene Deutsch has said, ". . . the masculinity complex is characterized by the predominance of active and aggressive tendencies that lead to conflict with the woman's environment and above all with the remaining feminine inner world . . . in its most primitive manifestation, masculinity appears as the direct enemy of feminine tendencies, disturbing their function."

Toni certainly fitted this description. However, she, like many other women with this kind of problem, was finally able to overcome her fear and envy of the male and to embrace her feminine nature without fear or shame.

Chapter 12

PSYCHIC FRIGIDITY

The problem of sexual promiscuity in women suffering from frigidity is a common one. Speaking in very general terms, it can be said to emanate from a desire to be sexually awakened. Women who seek a solution of this type feel that the next man will somehow break through the barrier that separates them from true sexual satisfaction, true relatedness, restore them to their erotic birthright. They are doomed to disappointment, of course, for an exterior solution of any permanent kind of this interior problem does not exist.

There is one form of promiscuity, however, that does not fit this above description. Basically it is not a search for the beloved but rather a deep, characterological tendency, closely allied to a curious and seemingly contradictory form of frigidity. The kind of woman who suffers from this disorder we have already characterized as the psychically frigid type. We have described this type as one which, if sexual reactions alone determined our definition, might be considered perfectly normal. The psychically frigid woman responds readily to sexual foreplay, and her orgasm is usually deep and satisfying. Examine her reactions as closely as we may, we can at first find no single aspect of them that would indicate a problem that could be classified as sexual frigidity.

However, the woman does have an obviously serious problem. She seems to be unable to form a close relationship that will endure. She is apparently devoted to an inner ideal of transiency in love. Sometimes she is not conscious of the fact that transiency in love is so important to her, but everything about her amorous career indicates this is so. She may select as partners married men or men who are chronically hostile to women and who always end up by rejecting them. Or she may do the rejecting herself. She is usually faithful to her partner of the moment and indeed sometimes pays lip service to the hope that this time the love affair will last. But just below the surface of her awareness she has no such wish. If the relationship shows any indication of moving toward permanency, she will create a reason for terminating it. And this is where her sexual problem shows: if she could not terminate it she would inevitably become sexually frigid with her partner.

One might wonder why I include this type here, since her problem is not one of physical frigidity as we ordinarily think of it—a primary blocking of sexual feeling, an inability to experience vaginal orgasm. I do so because in every case of this kind that I have treated there has been a profound sexual involvement. Early and destructive sexual experiences (usually some form of seduction) have led to a psychological inability to relate emotionally to another.

In the cases discussed up to now, we have seen that a too early experience can lead to a permanent repression of a child's entire sexual nature. Overstimulation leads to anxiety; anxiety leads to a ruthless repression of sensuality by the little individual. Basically the sexual experience has been felt as dangerous and unpleasant.

In our psychically frigid type we see, on the sexual level, just the opposite kind of conscious reaction. A too early stimulation causes a pleasurable sensual reaction, and the memory of this is held onto passionately. The deep guilt that is generated in the little girl, however, causes a displaced psychological reaction of great intensity.

To understand this personality structure more fully, let us look at a typical case.

Molly M. was a passionate bohemian in every sense of the word. When she first came to my office she was dressed in the height of what was then bohemian high fashion: dancing slippers, a dirndl-effect skirt and blouse, and long cotton stockings. She wore her hair in a pony tail and had no make up on whatsoever. She lived in Greenwich Village in a five-flight walk-up cold-water flat. She was then twenty-seven years old and had been living in the same place since her

graduation from college at twenty-two. She had a decent
job but preferred to stay in this exotic tenement.

Molly had come to me because, as she stated it, she was
scared. In the past two years she had become pregnant
twice and had had two abortions. The last one, which had
occurred three months before, had been performed under the most sordid circumstances; in the basement of a
tenement by a midwife with filthy hands. Performed without
anesthetic, it had been terribly painful and resulted in a
serious uterine infection which required hospitalization. In
the hospital the gynecologist had warned Molly that if she
had not already ruined her chances to have children she
might very well do so the next time. Despite her resolution at
that time to change her ways, she had recently picked up
with a penniless art student who obviously had no real feelings for Molly and, I suspected, no real ability to care for
any other person. It was clear that this relationship was going nowhere, just as the rest had.

But let us look at Molly's story.

Molly's mature sexual life had started at the age of thirteen! She had had an affair with a high school senior in her
home town—she described it as a "back-seat" affair—and
it had lasted for a year. From the beginning and even under the unfavorable circumstances that love-making in an
automobile must certainly create, Molly had had a total sexual
response.

Since that time she had had upward of forty sexual affairs. None of them had lasted for more than a year and
some only one or two weeks. All of them had been with men
who were ineligible for marriage either because they were already married or because they were not emotionally capable
of marrying.

Molly, though she had certain superficial pretensions to
being an intellectual, was not one by any means. But she
was an intelligent girl. She had a position as a researcher
on a weekly trade paper, and her work had put her in line
to become head of the research department. Her job represented the "respectable" side of her life. However, despite
some uneasiness of brief duration in college, she had never
seriously questioned the "rightness" of her sexual conduct.
Each time she had had an affair she believed that she was
in love and she never had more than one affair at a time.
When the current love was over she always experienced
feelings of relief.

If Molly had come from an environment where a free
attitude toward sexuality had prevailed, her actions might

not have seemed so inexplicable. But her home environment could not have been more conventional. She had come from a small New England city near Boston. Her father was the president of the leading bank in that city and had been active in church and civic affairs. Her mother, too, had been a church leader and a member of the school board. Her parents' marriage had obviously been a good one; the domestic life was serene; they rarely quarreled; their civic duties were most often shared enterprises. And they genuinely loved their three children. There were two girls older than Molly, and they had led most conventional lives. They had married after college and each had had two children.

What, then, had caused Molly's rebellion against her environment? And what was at the root of her inability to form a relationship? What was the cause of her psychic frigidity?

A psychiatrist familiar with this kind of case considers the possibility of an early seduction of some kind. It had indeed occurred.

Molly was unwilling to discuss it at first. And this was followed by an unwillingness to ascribe any particular significance to the event. She believed it was an isolated occurrence that had had no particular or permanent effect on her. Actually, as the matter unfolded, it became clear that this event was the very nucleus of her later difficulties.

It had happened when she was six. Three houses down from her there had lived a man in his early sixties. I shall call him Mr. Brown. He was a well-to-do person whose wife had died some years before and who now lived alone. He was very friendly, she remembered, with everyone, and often her father, out for an evening stroll, would drop in on him and spend an hour or two chatting on Mr. Brown's screened-in veranda. Occasionally he would come to Molly's house for dinner. She found out later that he was a director in her father's bank. He was certainly, as far as her parents or any other grownups were concerned, above all suspicion.

Sometimes Molly would play jump-rope or hopscotch outside of Mr. Brown's house. One day he invited her in and gave her a piece of cake and ten cents. She was delighted, and often thereafter he would have her in, always giving her something sweet to eat. He was pleasant and gentle and she loved him. She did not remember the first time it happened, but soon sitting on his lap became an integral part of her now frequent visits. He would tell her a story and ruffle her hair, touch her arms or hands. Gradually his touching extended to her legs and thighs. She liked the sensations and, being so young, she could not conceive of his doing anything that would be wrong.

Her visits now became almost daily occurrences, and then one day he touched her vagina. She could recall the whole event with great clarity. She remembered that his hand shook and that he looked very pale. Her sensations were exquisite and she involuntarily closed her thighs, pressing his hand against her vagina. At this point the whole "affair" became enormously exciting to her. For a period of almost a month she visited him as often as she could.

It is important to note that Mr. Brown did not confine his caresses to the little girl's clitoris. At length he actually penetrated her hymen with his finger. She remembered this because it was painful, but she also recalled that the sensations of pleasure outweighed the pain. Thereafter he would masturbate her vaginally whenever they met in his house.

This seduction lasted for some time, when one day while she was sitting on his lap he took his penis out and rubbed it against her. She was so initiated to the pleasures of sexuality by this time that the act did not seem strange to her, nor did the sight and size of a grown man's penis cause her the alarm it would normally occasion in a child. Her vagina was of course too small to admit more than a very partial entrance, but (and this she remembers clearly) though he did not thrust in any way, the little girl herself pressed her body toward him despite the pain it caused.

This occasion ended this bizarre and shocking experience. Apparently Mr. Brown was tardily overwhelmed by feelings of guilt or by a fear of getting caught, for he was not home when she next called for a visit and he did not return for over two years. By that time she had put the matter out of her conscious mind, or at least held the memory very much in abeyance.

This seduction was not difficult for Molly to recall, however, but she found it hard to recapture other feelings which had been associated with the experience, primarily the feeling of guilt.

Now let us take the matter step by step. Why, in the first place, did Molly react with excitement rather than shock to this whole experience? There are two reasons. In the first place, the seduction was done by a person who was loved by the child. He was a friend of the family, no less acceptable or trustworthy to the little girl than her own father and mother.

In the second place, Molly had not yet passed completely through the stage of infantile sexuality into the latency period, when normally sex goes underground until puberty. She was still able to be excited by sensual experiences. A year or two later she might not have accepted the situation, probably would have reacted to it with shock or horror; it might have contributed to a different kind of frigidity, perhaps the anesthesia of total frigidity.

It was clear, however, that she *had* felt guilty about her reactions. She had not communicated the experience to her parents—a clear indication of guilt feelings. And later she had separated the seduction and its sensual pleasures from her conscious mind, made no connection between it and her later unconventional behavior. If she had not experienced guilt she would have had to make no such separation.

While Molly had no further sexual experiences in her latency period, she began to behave differently from the other girls in her group very early. At twelve she began to pet with a boy next door and was certain that she would have had intercourse with him had he not been so frightened of her advances. At thirteen she would sneak out at night to meet one of several older boys, and on one of these occasions she had sexual intercourse. She went around with this boy for about a year. He then graduated from high school and went away to college, and Molly promptly started another sexual relationship with another senior in high school.

Sexual affairs from then on followed one after the other through high school and college. The only concession Molly made to conventional morality was the afore-mentioned fact that she did not allow the affairs to overlap.

As she entered her teens another aspect of Molly's behavior became apparent. More and more she sought out individuals markedly different from those on her own social level. By fifteen she had become distinctly "wild," coming in late at night and refusing to obey her parents in any way. She would not go out with any of the high school or college boys she met. She had made friends with a group of girls on a lower economic level whose social life consisted largely of picking up men at dances. In this way Molly met several men who played in bands and who were, of course, not what her family could possibly have approved of. She did not care in the least; she felt, she told me, "unutterably bored" with her family, felt "they were sunk in their way of life," led absolutely "joyless and pointless existences."

Despite all this, Molly maintained her scholastic record at a high level and was admitted to college—another sign of the division within her personality. In college her unremitting affairs persisted, as did her selection of friends outside of her own social sphere. At one point she had an affair with a Negro labor organizer, at another with an Italian dock hand, at still another with the father of a college classmate. It is not surprising, then, that as soon as she finished college (and here, too, she maintained her good scholastic record) she gravitated toward Greenwich Village and immediately launched into a bohemian social and sexual existence. She experienced no conscious regrets or qualms of conscience as, year in, year out, she continued in this mode of living, a mode so different from that of her parents. She was sustained by her pride in what she called her "healthy animality" and was fond of stating that most people led lives of great frustration and "of quiet desperation."

Her animosity toward her parents did not diminish when she grew up, and at the time she came to see me she had not visited them for two years.

The consequences of Molly's early seduction, as you can see, *were* grave. However, the psychological structure she had developed to cope with this seduction is not a hard one to understand.

Human beings are largely guided by the pleasure principle, and this is most clearly evinced in childhood. Molly had received a great deal of pleasure from her early sexual experience, but she had also experienced a great deal of guilt about it. When Mr. Brown departed she had entered her latency period. But when puberty, with its reassertion of sexuality, set in, the original sexual experience had set a mold for Molly's personality. She enjoyed and sought sex to an abnormal degree for her tender years.

In her unconscious life, however, she felt guilty for these feelings. Because of her precocious sensuality her problem then was to get rid of her guilt feelings so that she could indulge her sexuality. This meant, in effect, getting rid of her parents for, in childhood, guilt of this kind is always associated with parental prohibition. She did this by denying that her parents had any importance to her, by repressing all warm feelings toward them, by constructing a set of values in which they were, to use her words again, "stupid," "loveless squares," "without a drop of sensuality."

As Molly and I continued our examination of her life and feelings it became apparent that the erection of this defensive mechanism had cost a great deal indeed, even in terms of those pleasures to which she was devoted. In order to be enjoyed, sex had to partake of the nature of the original seduction; it had to be a forbidden and guilty act; it had to be with a person who was, in her mind, anathema to her parents. And, primarily, it could not move over into a permanent and abiding relationship, for if it did it could no longer be considered forbidden and guilty.

This meant, of course, that love could never lead to marriage or to children and to the joys these bring. For if a man was respectable, "meant well by her," loved her, in her unconscious life she would immediately associate him with her parents and their approval, and this would kill all sexual feeling in her. She would be frigid with him.

There was, of course, deep anxiety underneath Molly's rebellion against a permanent relationship. During the course of our work together and after she had begun to see the implications of her problem, she began to try to associate with men who were more eligible for a decent relationship. A dream she had during the course of her first attempt at such a relationship (with a young doctor she had met) shows the problem quite clearly.

In this dream she is sitting in the back seat of a car, kissing a young man in an intern's uniform. She is very excited as they kiss and decides that she will have intercourse with him. At this point the young intern says, "Please marry me." No sooner are the words out of his mouth than she begins to feel terrified, as though something awful is going to happen. She begins to tremble and wants to get out of the car and run, but she is so frightened that she cannot move. Suddenly she sees the face of a man outside the car. He is dressed in evening clothes and has a large dollar sign on his hat. He points a gun at them and says very clearly, "Both of you must die." At that point she woke up in an absolute panic which lasted for over an hour.

The intern in the dream stands, of course, for the young doctor she knows. The man with the dollar sign on his hat stands for her banker father. Sex is all right, and she wishes for it as long as it is furtive and hidden. The moment it becomes respectable ("Please marry me") the hidden and guilty act will be made known and her father will punish her in the most horrible way possible.

She had, as you can see, never resolved her early guilt

feelings about the childhood seduction. Her whole life had been built around this early experience.

Molly's relationship with the young doctor did not prosper, but in the course of our work she finally did meet and marry a very fine man. On the basis of insights she had had, she had decided to postpone intercourse with him until after the marriage. When the love-making began she at first responded sexually, but in a matter of a few weeks she became quite frigid.

This reaction of course represented, as in the case of the intern, her lifelong fear. However, since she had faced up to her psychological frigidity, had stopped running away into pointless and meaningless relationships, the resolution of this problem was merely a matter of time, of "working through" the guilt feelings she had never dared to face before.

The form of psychic frigidity represented by Molly's case has always, in my experience, been caused by a childhood seduction. The seduction usually takes place between the fourth and seventh year, and the child reacts to the experience with strong sensual pleasure accompanied by guilt. This guilt is handled by a withdrawal from the parents and from values they represent. And sensual pleasure becomes an end in itself, dissociated from friendly perduring relations with another person. It must be furtive, indulged in with unlikely persons; acute anxiety develops if there is any danger that it will lead to marriage.

The seduction need not be as complete or as direct as Molly's. I have had a case in which a single sight of grownups having sexual intercourse has had the effect of a seduction on a child. In such a case the pleasure reaction becomes associated with the early erotic feelings toward the father. The suggestion in the child's mind is that her "evil" wishes can be granted if she will displace them onto another person. In later years this becomes the model for sexual behavior; sexual desire in the woman is too closely associated with the father image, so the love object sought must be as different from the father image as possible.

Sometimes "liberal" parents seduce their children quite unwittingly. Not too long ago it became the practice among certain "liberated" or intellectual families to indulge in a species of nudism within the home. This practice was based on a misunderstanding of certain contributions of modern psychology, mainly the concept of inhibition. The parents wished to prevent their children from being inhibited or prudish about the human body. Such parents made no difficulty about parading around nude in front of sons and daughters of any age.

Parents who believe in this manner have rather elaborate rationales and present them convincingly. If certain of my patients are an indication, however, I can testify that many children do not have the "healthy" reaction to nudism in the home that the parents had expected. To a six-year-old girl the sight of a naked father can be far too stimulating an experience for her to handle. She will react either with shock or excitement or both. The same is true of boys who are permitted to view their mothers in the nude.

We have seen that erotic fixation on parents constitutes a stage in the growth process. Whatever it may be in other societies, primitive or otherwise, nudity in our society is associated with lustful feelings. Family nudism, I firmly believe, tends to fixate children on parents permanently by causing unnecessary stimulation and hence strong guilt feelings. The result can be similar to a direct seduction of the child.

Psychic frigidity is often confused with a temporal emotional condition we call situational frigidity. A woman suffering from situational frigidity has no basic sexual problem. Her responses have always been normal and her orgasm is both frequent and satisfying. However, some severe reality problem has arisen in her life which has caused a temporary eclipse of her sexual responsiveness.

On occasion a woman may become quite disturbed by this fact. Let me give an example.

Anne S. was thirty-five. She had had a happy marriage for ten years. In the first seven years of her marriage she had had two children, both girls. She had had no more fears of pregnancy and motherhood than she had had of sex. Her upbringing had been, from the psychiatric standpoint, exemplary. In every determinable way she was an excellent sweetheart, mother, and wife.

Six months before she came to see me she had given birth to her third child, a boy. In a very short time it became clear that the child was mongoloid. After several weeks of indecision she had finally yielded to the pressure of the doctor and her husband and the child had been committed to an institution. At the time she came to me she had just learned that its congenital defects would be fatal within two or three months.

When Anne had resumed her sexual relationship with her husband after the birth of this child she had been completely unresponsive and actively disliked the whole act. This had upset her. She had thought this would pass in a week or two, but it had not. The fear that she may have lost her capacity to love or at least to love her husband had brought her to a psychiatrist.

Anne could not have been more mistaken about the significance of her unresponsiveness. She had underestimated the depth of the blow the birth of such a child can have on a mother. Grief and other profound emotions incapacitate the ability to love; one's entire confidence in oneself is shaken. It is perfectly normal under such circumstances to withdraw emotionally. In fact, it is even desirable. Wounded feelings must heal, and immobilizing oneself emotionally is good therapeutic procedure.

Time is the only anodyne for this kind of normal emotional pull-back. In this case Anne's child died within two months, as had been predicted. Her so-called situational frigidity lasted for three months after that and then disappeared entirely.

Since the sexuality of women, as we have seen, is so "psychological" in its nature, these temporary situational frigidities are probably quite prevalent, though there are no final statistics on them. They can be caused by a wide variety of circumstances and can last for a week or two to several months, depending on the severity of the circumstance. I have seen this type of temporary frigidity brought on by such disparate causes as the death of a loved parent, the illness of a child (even a relatively slight illness), a husband's economic worries, and a difficult birth, to name but a few.

One very scrupulous wife, who took great pride in her ability to drive a car, even had a sexual blocking for a few nights when she was given her first traffic ticket. She had parked too long on the wrong side of the street, and the officer who gave her the ticket had also given her a stern talking-to.

All one really has to know about situational frigidity is that it isn't serious and that it's well within the normal range of woman's delicately balanced sexual nature and will most certainly pass. The only therapy one needs is patience.

These cases represent, then, the major forms of frigidity. My intent in presenting them has been threefold. In the first place, it is important to understand what type of frigidity you have. Second, it can be helpful to see the individual characteristics of each kind of frigidity. Third, it is necessary to understand that all of the frigidities have certain basic characteristics in common (with the exception of situational frigidity), for this latter fact will allow us to approach each individual type with one basic form of solution.

With this final information in mind we are now ready to turn our attention to the means by which frigidity can be resolved.

Chapter 13

THE POWER OF LOVE

We have come now to the last and most important part of our journey together, to the point where we can examine the means by which real love can be achieved. Let us start by examining what real love is, its role in life and its component parts.

Because of their problems in loving, many people arrive at a point where they turn against love itself. Having lost their hope of achieving love, they quite humanly tend to depreciate it, try to minimize its importance. One of the commonest statements I hear from frigid patients in the first interview goes something like this: "Well, it really doesn't matter, I suppose; there aren't very many happy marriages anyway. And I suppose there are more important things than love."

Let us correct any tendency of this kind right here and now.

Using the word in its widest sense, I would say that the ability to love is the single most important characteristic that man has. It is the faculty upon which all the great actions, hopes, and aspirations of the world are founded. Without it there could be no brotherhood among men, and therefore the very concept of civilization as we understand it would be unknown, even unthinkable. Men would be essentially isolated individuals whose personal drives, needs, and appetites would be the only realities to them. Aloneness, a terrible loneliness (those who cannot love will know what I mean), would be mankind's lot.

Love means, in its very deepest sense, union; union between individuals, between women and women, men and men, men and women. It is the most basic and profound urge we have, and its power for good is illimitable.

In love we make the good of our partner (whether he is our child, our neighbor, or our sweetheart) as important to us as our own good. In the union of love we are able to experience the essential oneness of man and nature, to know that the universe is indeed our home and all men within it members of our family. In this way man learns through love that he is not alone, not condemned to the pain and anxiety he experiences when he has nobody with whom he can share his mind, his heart, his body.

The concept of this happy unity is most clearly seen in the love between men and women. The act of sexual love is a direct expression of it. Two individuals once unknown to each other, until recently total strangers, now nevertheless literally merge together physically, know each other in the closest of physical embraces. They were miraculously made for this purpose, constructed for this union. The man leaves something of himself within the woman, his sperm. And a part of the woman joins this, merges with it. They have indeed become one flesh.

And this merging, in addition to the joy and comfort it brings to each to join with the other as one, can become a creative act. From the union a child may be created. Thus we see that the profound result of the union which always characterizes love is productivity, creation.

If this physical coupling were all there was, it would be miraculous still, though an experience shared by other than human forms of life. But man, as distinct from animals, has mind. And minds, as well as bodies, have the capacity to merge too, the need to, the profound joy in so doing. It is when body and mind of a man and woman merge, become a unity, that we see the highest expression of what we term love.

When two people are able to join as one in love, there are certain very definite things that happen to them, as far as each individual mind is concerned.

In the first place, each is able to come far closer to his or her own potentialities. The merging that takes place in psychological love is essentially creative (just as its physical counterpart is), and so each lover is able to come closer and closer to his true self. All who have ever loved know of this inward blossoming, this fecundation by the love of the other. In work, in play, in all the inner and outer activities of life, the individual becomes far more vital and more productive than before.

Another important aspect of love: to each, as I have said, the love partner becomes as important as oneself, and from this it follows that the good of the loved one is all important to the other. Thus all things that help the other, cause him to be joyful, secure, freely and completely himself, become a chief concern of the other. This fact is why real love never leads to domination or to a struggle for power between two people. Through the mersion of love the uniqueness and individuality of the other person becomes precious, and hence all effort is made to guard the special qualities of the beloved. In love we never encounter a man trampling on his wife's rights and needs or a woman competing with her husband. The value of the other as he is and as he can grow to be becomes the highest value in life.

Because of the high value she places upon her loved one a woman makes the understanding of him one of her most important activities. And this understanding furthers love, which in turn furthers understanding, so that the process is a very dynamic one. By gaining a knowledge of her loved one she is able ultimately to go to the very root of his personality, thus making an even deeper merging of her with him possible. Such understanding implies, of course, a great sensitivity to all of his reactions. And it makes her, too, inquire urgently (and creatively) into herself, so that no blocks to their deep psychological communion can develop.

These are, then, some of the results of real love. I have listed them as a rebuttal of and a reminder to any who have, through repeated defeat, become discouraged in their struggles to love and have tended therefore to minimize love's importance. There is nothing in life that is so important as love. In fact, as one of my patients once said, looking back on the period when she was unable to love, "Without love there is nothing in life."

One cannot win the battle to love if one minimizes it. The frigid woman, above all, must realize this and never give up her struggle. Indeed, a complete awareness of how important love is can be in itself a big step along the way to achieving the ability to love and to be loved.

Now if we summarize what has just been said about love, what do we find is its essential characteristic? This: the ability to see the other person *as he is* and to esteem him above

everything else for his individual quality, indeed to love him
(and so want to merge with him) for it.

On the other hand, if we were to summarize all the case
histories of the various forms of frigidity I have given and
all the other pertinent facts I have adduced about frigidity,
we would find just the opposite fact. The frigid woman, of
whatever variety she may be, *never sees the man she wants
to love as he is.* His individual and essential quality is entirely unknown to her and unknowable by her. He is a
series of projections from her past. He is a composite of the
fears, the errors, the misunderstandings of her infancy and
childhood. The real union of love is therefore impossible
with this quasi monster she has conjured up.

Thus we can see that the major task of the frigid woman
is to rid herself of these projections she makes upon mankind
in general and upon her own man in particular. She must
see through them and divest herself of them, come to see
men in their true role vis-à-vis woman and her husband in
all his uniqueness and with all his potentiality.

That is step one.

When she has done this there is another step she must
take. If one thinks of the description of love I have given,
one realizes that it implies a very great security within oneself, an acceptance of one's own uniqueness and essential
femininity. But the frigid woman fears and rejects femininity, as we have seen, feeling it to be a dangerous trap. She
must learn to alter this basic and negative attitude entirely.
She must see how childish and false, how utterly self-depriv-
ing this view of womanhood is and give it up.

Thus we see that in frigidity the two main doors to psychological and sexual union—to love, in short—have been
closed and locked.

If these two doors can be opened again, the frigid woman
will have resolved her problem.

Just these two doors? Is this not an oversimplification?
To these two questions I can give unequivocal answers: yes
to the first and no to the second. These are the two roots of
the problem. Attack them head on, resolve them, and the
major part of the task has been done.

Chapter 14

STEPS TO FREEDOM

The resolution of an emotional problem is a process, a process with a beginning, a middle, and an end. To put this process in motion and to maintain it in motion, two distinct approaches are necessary.

The first step is to grasp the problem *objectively* to understand its nature, its implications, to learn all the *outside* facts about it one can grasp with one's intellect.

We have now taken this first step, an all-important one for most people. If you have read thus far, you have learned a great many objective facts about frigidity.

You have learned what it is and the toll it exacts; you have seen why women are subject to it and how it originates in the individual and the different forms it may take. You have seen, too, how woman has attempted to masculinize her personality, how she has tried to eschew sex entirely; and you have seen why these unhappy attempts *can* be successful, why they are inherent biological and psychological possibilities.

This kind of objective understanding is of great importance. It frees one from prejudice and prevents one from seeking false solutions (which abound); it brings one face to face with the real nature of the dilemma of frigidity, its essentially psychological structure, and it uncovers the hidden area where personal responsibility lies.

Without this kind of objective intellectual understanding the individual woman could not come to direct grips with frigidity, for she would not know its nature. This type of knowledge, then, has carried us to the very edge of the bridge to true womanhood.

In order to cross it, however, the individual woman must do more than merely understand in an objective manner.

The second and all-important step in the resolution of the problem of frigidity requires a *subjective* approach, an inquiry by the individual woman into the attitudes and emotions that are preventing her from achieving maturity. The kind of knowledge one gains in this way we call insight. If one can get true insight into the attitudes and feelings upon which one's own frigidity is based, the problem can be completely resolved.

At the moment this may seem like a big order and insight a frightening word. Every woman knows how complex her emotions are, how difficult to understand, how multi-faceted every human being is.

But I wish to tell you now, at the outset, that the whole approach can be kept very simple. Frigidity is like a log jam on a narrow stream. If two or three logs jam together, forming a barrier, all the other logs will jam up behind them, forming a complicated maze that stretches backward sometimes for miles. To release the jam, however, all one has to do is to free the first two or three logs, and then the others will resume their unimpeded journey.

The emotional log jam we call frigidity is held in place by two basically neurotic attitudes. The first is an attitude toward men; the second is an attitude toward real womanhood. We have seen these attitudes in every form of frigidity and have seen how they function. If the individual woman can come to grips with these two attitudes in herself, if she can dislodge them, the free flow of her personality toward health and maturity will resume once again. Insight can dislodge these hindering attitudes and keep them dislodged.

Let us start, then, and see how insight into these attitudes can be achieved by the frigid woman.

The first thing you must do is a very practical one. You must give yourself, at least at the beginning, a certain amount of time alone, absolutely alone, each day. It might be for ten minutes or for a half hour or an hour, but you must be alone and you must seek this time regularly. It is most helpful if you can select a time when your mind is relatively free of worries and duties.

What do you do to achieve insight at these junctures? You start, on the simplest level possible, to let yourself *really feel* your negative emotions about your husband or sweetheart. Your only aim at this point is to let these negative feelings come to the surface, to seek them out, experience them *to the full*.

Pick out some small but recurrent irritation or annoyance he causes you; the more trifling, the better. Fix on it, then dare to allow your emotions and thoughts about it to hold sway.

Let me give you a single example from the case history of a frigid patient. Every day this woman's husband, on rising, dressed in the bathroom. He invariably left his razor on the sink and his pajamas in an untidy heap in a corner. This had irritated her and she had spoken about it to him several times; he would reform for a few days but then would invariably fall back into his old habits.

This bit of information about their married life had been presented quite casually in the course of my first discussion with this patient. At that time she spoke of this peccadillo of her husband's as a minor annoyance. A bit later, when she had returned to the subject for the third time, each time expressing annoyance, I encouraged her to dwell on it, to let herself feel the full measure of her emotions about it. I told her that I suspected there was a good deal more in her *feelings* about this apparently trifling matter than she suspected and that I thought this because she had brought it up so many times.

At first she protested that the matter was too small to pay attention to; that there were more important things to consider. But with encouragement she gradually allowed herself to pursue her true feelings. Underneath her commonplace protest was, as I had thought, an emotional cave-of-the-four-winds.

Her husband's "sloppy actions," it turned out, did not merely "annoy" her; they "enraged" her. In her words, they signified his desire "to humiliate me"; "he thinks I have nothing to do but pick up after him, to wait on him hand and foot." Her anger became more and more explosive as she reflected on the matter, and it led very quickly and directly to her underlying attitude toward men as a whole. Men wanted to do nothing more or less than to enslave women, to exploit them. They considered themselves a race apart, superior to women. All they wanted from a woman was sex, or anything else they could get out of them. And they were powerful, and thus dangerous; if a woman really showed her hostility they would use their physical strength against her. And so it went, on and on, the stored-up rage and the hostile and frightened attitudes that lay just beneath the surface and constituted the very bricks and mortar of her frigidity.

In pursuing this technique for getting at one's feelings it is best always to select, as in the example quoted, one or more of the petty annoyances in everyday life. Does your husband's behavior in company embarrass you? Has he an annoying habit? (Bathroom habits of a mate are very fruitful sources for this kind of self-investigation.) Is he untidy? Does his taste in clothes irritate you? Does he ignore the children or pay too much attention to them, ignoring you? You will know what has become the provocative agent in your life; select it and explore the feelings underneath it to their limit.

As you let your feeling come to the surface, please note how quickly you move from contemplation of your husband's annoying characteristic to very broad generalities about men. In the case above the woman moved almost at once from annoyance, to rage, to ascribing a hidden motive to all men—a desire to enslave women, to exploit them.

It was the generalities she made which (in the end) revealed to her with great clarity that her underlying attitude created a spiritual climate in which real love and therefore a productive marriage were virtually impossible. How can one love, in any real sense, a person one regards, basically, as a tyrant?

Taking this highly emotional inventory cannot be a swift affair. In the beginning, for the first several sessions with herself, a frigid woman may find that no very strong feelings or passionate generalizations will come up. But if she perseveres she will inevitably get to an area where the feelings are intense and negative indeed. We have found that such feelings always exist in frigidity. If they did not, there would be no frigidity.

The frigid woman has hidden the intensity of such feelings from her conscious mind for two reasons. To know these reasons can help you, make you somewhat braver in your attempt to surface the feelings.

The first reason these emotions have remained hidden is their very intensity. They were, in the beginning, felt to be overwhelming; it was as if they proceeded from a bottomless well of feeling. And so, through the years, one has learned to hide them, even from oneself, to fix them on trifles in order to minimize them—to deny that, indeed, they exist at all.

Only by letting them up into the awareness can one experience the fact that their intensity is *not* overwhelming and that the emotion one experiences has very definite limits; it does not proceed from a bottomless well.

I recall one woman who, in approaching this problem, would not let herself weep over a strong underlying feeling of rejection by men that she had partially uncovered in herself. "If I start crying I feel I'll never stop," she told me. She was not being histrionic either; that's the way she really felt. When she did let herself cry, however, the storm lasted for a mere thirty minutes or so—and then it was done with for good. She was terribly relieved to find that the emotion which, when unexpressed, seemed so boundless had very concrete limits. From that point on she was much more at home with all of her emotions, not nearly so frightened of them.

The second reason a woman fears to let her feelings about her husband (and men in general) come to the surface is that she believes that the things she feels are literally true. They exist in her unconscious or partly conscious mind as profound convictions. She holds them at bay because she does not wish to face just how completely a part of her mind believes that her highly irrational feelings are based on reality.

It will help, however, to know that, no matter how convinced a part of you is that your negative feelings represent reality, such is not the case. Your investigation is not going to prove that your hidden fears are valid; it is going to prove that they are invalid. These deep and hidden convictions are shaped early in a woman's life, primarily by her relationships with her parents and secondarily through her relationships with her brothers and sisters. They are basically irrational feelings, erected as defenses against childhood and girlhood fears and misunderstandings. They have no real basis in fact; they do not pertain to the male *as he is*.

It is of very great importance to know this when you begin to uncover your most secret convictions. No matter how real these negative attitudes appear to be, remember that they are *only* feelings, not reality. As long as you keep that fact in the forefront of your mind you will increasingly dare to let these feelings up into your awareness, into your conscious mind.

I counsel women to be remorseless with themselves in this search for any negative feelings they might possess toward their husband and toward all men. Do not stop when you have seen one or two details that indicate an amount of feeling you had not clearly known you possessed. Press onward and inward fearlessly until you have exposed every last hostile and irrational emotion and attitude you have.

One woman who came to me had worked very hard for five sessions on her negative feelings toward men. We had started our mutual investigation when she confessed that any slight irritability on her husband's part caused her to feel extremely anxious, often resulted in actual nausea.

We pursued the matter and soon found a great store of antagonism toward men hidden just beneath the surface of an apparently gentle person. She had, we discovered, the common, classical conviction that men wish to exploit women, to bend them to their wills. She soon realized she had been interpreting many everyday happenings in the light of this belief. Her husband, an editor, sometimes had to work at home in the evening and had asked her to keep the television set low until he was finished. Though she knew his homework was exacting, she took this to be a characteristic infringement of her "rights" and had a great deal of stored-up rage about it. She also had hidden rage at such commonplace duties as bringing his clothes to the cleaner, entertaining his business friends, cleaning his "filthy" study, etc.

We explored them all, one by one. Neither of us, however, felt that we had come to the end of the matter. There was something that eluded us. She as well as I felt certain of that. We persisted, therefore, and the hidden feeling at last showed itself. Returning to her first complaint, I asked her if she had ever been physically struck by her husband.

"No," she replied, "but I often *feel* that he is going to strike me."

Knowing her husband to be a kind person, I pursued the matter, and it soon developed that she had a very strong unconscious conviction that men in general had no compunction whatever about using their superior physical strength against women to obtain what they wanted. In other words, she not only felt that men were basically hostile to women but that they were potentially extremely violent.

This was a bizarre conviction, and my patient soon realized its irrational nature. Her picture of men was based on early memories of a truly sadistic father; he had frequently struck her mother. When she realized the pervasive importance of this only slightly repressed physical fear of men she was able to resume a psychological growth that had been severely impeded from the earliest age.

But the point I wish to emphasize is that she had to persist in her search for hidden attitudes. If she had assumed that she had gotten to the heart of her difficulty by uncovering the first few negative feelings, her self-investigation could not have succeeded. Please mark the fact that she did not *feel* she had come to the end of her emotional inventory until she had actually done so. If one is honest with oneself one can sense, feel, when important attitudes still lie hidden within.

If you persist in your daily sessions with yourself, however, the time will come when you will feel that you have exposed to your own view all of your angry feelings and your negative attitudes toward men, come to the very lees of the feelings left over from childhood. You have now made a major step toward recovery. The biggest log in the jam has been removed.

Why does this necessarily follow?

One of the major contributions of modern psychiatry has been the establishment of the fact that attitudes and feelings have the power to do lasting harm only when they are hidden from one's awareness, or half hidden from it. The frigid woman's troubling vestiges of youthful error, once they have been made conscious, automatically lose the greater part of their power to do harm. When they become known to the conscious mind they are then exposed to judgment, reason, and further information. They are seen, by one's intelligence, to be fragile balloons of easily exploded ignorance. When this happens, the natural movement of the personality toward health, blocked for years by hidden fears, rages, defenses, false attitudes, is resumed.

A woman who can achieve this is now *prepared* to understand her husband *as he is*—and all other men *as man is*. If you will recall, that particular ability, to comprehend and care about the uniqueness of one's mate, is a chief prerequisite for love.

If the frigid woman did not explore her irrational feelings in the manner I have described, any objective information about men, learned from whatever source, would be useless. Her *hidden* feelings about men would still dominate. Now, however, with the hidden feelings up and out, she is ready to hear more about men as they really are, to contrast the reality to her projection upon it. We shall take that latter step in the next chapter, but before we do there is another, further insight into one's feeling, which it will be very helpful to achieve.

Women who suffer from frigidity often have, in addition to negative feelings toward the male sex, another very marked characteristic. They are subject to powerful *fantasies* which militate against the recovery of their lost sexuality and their psychological maturation. It is extremely important that these fantasies be ruthlessly explored and exploded. If they are not, they serve the unhappy function of preserving the unhealthy conviction that one deserves a far better fate than that of being a beloved wife and mother.

Such fantasies are often half hidden from view, just as are one's negative feelings about men. They are daydreams left over from adolescence or earlier. Their destructive power derives from the fact that the daydreamer either still believes that the dreams are realizable or that she could have achieved them if her husband and family had not prevented her from doing so.

It is amazing how powerful and persistent these fantasies can be. They generally spring from an early desire to become an actress, a dancer, or a concert artist. However, they may also express wishes to become a doctor, lawyer, athlete, diplomat, or whatever. Their impossible, Walter-Mittyish character is blithely ignored by the daydreamer. I have had frigid women of forty and even fifty, who, just beneath the logical, sound surface of their minds, still believed that someday (tomorrow perhaps, next year certainly) they would go to acting school and soon obtain leading roles in a Broadway drama, or resume their piano lessons and become famous concert artists.

Such fantasies derive their power from the fact that the daydreamer feels unable to deal with reality. Since a woman who is frigid *is* dealing with her real-life situation in an inadequate manner, it is not strange that she should hold onto such fantasies with passion. They protect her from her feelings of inferiority. What matter, says her unconscious mind, if you are unable to love; what matter if your husband exploits you, attempts to enslave you. Tomorrow—someday, at any rate—you will show them all that you are beautiful, glamorous, a great performer, or doctor, or lawyer, or Indian chief.

The frigid woman should approach such fantasies in the same manner as she approaches her negative feelings toward the male sex. First she should let the fantasy have full play. She should allow herself to imagine herself as impresario, doctor, whatever fantastic dream her unconscious has fixed on. Let the daydream roll on and on. Note its magnitude, its grandiose quality, its glitter and its glamor.

When all the details of the fantasy have been experienced, allow yourself to imagine what life would be like for you if you were *never* able to realize any single aspect of this daydream. If you feel depressed by such a prospect, if the contemplation of life without the possibility of realizing such a dream of glory seems empty, you have had an important experience. You have taken your fantasy's full measure. You now can get some idea of what an important part it plays in your emotional life.

Do not be afraid of the depression, the feeling of emptiness that will come with your first conscious attempts to free yourself of your fantasy. It can be the beginning of a far richer emotional life than any which depends on an unrealizable daydream. Therefore, persist for a few days in imagining what life will be like if you do not ever realize your daydream. Please notice that your depression does not go beyond a certain depth and that it is not incapacitating; also note that your feeling of deprivation is not unendurable.

I am not using auto-suggestion in these last remarks. A persistent daydream has certain characteristics in common with a drug or alcohol habituation. The daydreamer has, over a long period of time, learned to handle reality in terms of her drug—her deep-seated daydream. Without realizing it she has come to feel that, without this psychological narcotic, life would be impossible. She must, in a very real sense, wean herself from it, gradually realize that life without it is not nearly so dreary, so difficult, as she had imagined it would be.

The next step in the process is to explode the day dream entirely. This can be done with a few pinpricks of cold logic. Most people, realizing that such daydreams, formed in the heat of youth, have no function in reality, have long ago given them up in favor of living as passionately as possible in the present. The frigid woman, however, having a reason for keeping them alive, has never scrutinized them in the cold light of rationality.

I know of one woman who, at the age of thirty-eight, with three children under fifteen years of age, still felt she could become a dancer. As she looked more closely at this conviction she became increasingly surprised at how seriously she really took this fantasy. At length, when she felt really ready to face sacrificing her lifelong fantasy, she wrote a list of facts and questions. I present them here.

1. To become a dancer I would have to study the dance for a minimum of five years; during that time I would have to practice dancing for about eight hours a day. Could I take this discipline?

2. If my mind were able to take such discipline would my body be able to stand up under such arduous work?

3. If I were able to arrange it would I be willing to give up my daily contact and relationship with my three children?

4. If I overcame every obstacle and became a well-known dancer, achieving my wildest dream of success, I would have to go on tour for at least eight months of the year; this would mean separation from my husband and children during that time. Do I want this? Even if I do, could I take it emotionally?

The answers to these questions were obviously passionate noes. And the result of such a common-sensical examination of her long-standing fantasy was, at long length, freedom from it.

It will not take much logical thought to dispose of your daydreams, thus clearing the way to a life in the passionate present rather than in a mythical future. Ask yourself the kinds of questions indicated above and give yourself honest answers.

In giving the case histories of women suffering from the various forms and degrees of frigidity, I have described to some extent the early origins of their problems. I should now like to raise the question of just how much knowledge of one's early, often buried, experiences one must uncover to achieve feminine maturity.

In my opinion, the majority of women suffering from frigidity do *not* have to go into the matter of their childhood experiences to any extent at all. The evidence that their childhood experiences *were* traumatic to some degree is contained in the fact that they do have problems in the present. It is always the immediate problem about which people develop their deepest and strongest emotions. The technique of "feeling" one's way through one's problem is, as I have said, the method that really works with frigidity; it is one's present emotions, therefore, that constitute the major material of one's self-examination.

Actually understanding present feelings and attitudes reveals the past, for it was in the past that these attitudes were established; they have changed very little since their inception.

Why, then, did I go into the detailed childhood development of frigidity in my case histories? For the same reason that I gave all the other objective facts about frigidity before we approached this section. The more conscious knowledge one has of the entire problem of frigidity, the more one dares to face up to the responsibility for one's own problem— and the more one is *able* to face up to it also. For knowledge can free one of the ignorance and superstition upon which resistance to achieving psychic maturity is based.

I am not, on the other hand, holding that there is any fundamental objection to a scrutiny of early experiences or to helpful speculation about them. Sometimes, as in the case of an early seduction, or a rape that is remembered, early experiences can throw a therapeutic sidelight on one's present feelings. However, the myriad details that go into the formation of everyone's personality while growing up can be confusing if one tries to understand them all without the help of an expert guide; and it is not requisite for recovery to understand them all. So if self-examination of one's early experiences does not seem to be immediately helpful, I would abandon it entirely; I would confine myself to a "feeling through" of my problem in the present, undoing the harm the childhood attitudes are still causing in the here and now.

The steps for achieving insight into one's negative emotions which I recommend here are the most difficult steps one has to take on the road to maturity. If you can take them, the hardest part will be over. The remaining part of the process of recovery occurs rather naturally, is a matter of acquiring more information, allowing new feelings to grow and expand inside oneself, accepting guidance past a few possible pitfalls. You will see what I mean as we continue in the following chapters.

Chapter 15

THE MALE SEX: A NEW HORIZON

The self-exploration described in the last chapter results in the surfacing of hidden feelings, attitudes, and fantasies. Getting them up and out, exposing them to the bright light of reason and judgment, clears the psychological atmosphere almost miraculously.

The next most helpful step to take, I have found, is a re-evaluation of the male sex. The woman who suffers from frigidity has, by definition, very little knowledge of what men are really like. Since her attitudes toward men were formed in her distant past and have altered little through the years, she has a child's-eye view of men. To her, as parents to a child, men are powers, not people. Projecting her own childhood fears and hopes and needs upon them, she has been calling that reality and acting accordingly.

This next step, the conscious revaluation of men, can be achieved by learning what the male sex is really like—how it differs from the female sex, what makes men think, act, and feel the way they do in everyday life—and by contrasting this knowledge with the negative attitudes and feelings she has now brought to the surface of her mind. In this way she will soon learn to understand her husband *as he is*, and thus achieve the ability to love him in all of his uniqueness and individuality.

The central characteristic of the male, and the one that most clearly differentiates him from the female, is his aggressiveness.

In the sexual sphere this shows itself most clearly in the fact that the man takes, for the most part, the initiative in wooing. He it is who is the pursuer, the girl the pursued; he it is who proposes and he it is who initiates sex.

An analogy to this fundamentally aggressive activity of the male in relationship to the female is seen, in a primordial biological form, by the function of his sperm. As you may know, the individual spermatozoon is an individual cell which is propelled by a microscopic tail. After the deposit of spermatozoa in the vagina, the individual sperm *actively* seeks out and joins the ova, which has been *passively* waiting for it. This physiological metaphor, according to certain leading theoreticians, well expresses the fundamentally aggressive nature of man in relationship to woman, psychologically as well as sexually.

The male's aggressiveness is, in general, directed to mastery of the outside world. It shows in him from his earliest years. The sports that he selects have to do with physical aggression almost exclusively (of course some girls also like certain aggressive sports at an early age, but most give them up in puberty). He likes the sports in which he has to run hard, to charge, to tackle, throw, and hit. In his adolescence he will spend years in mastering skills that concern such aggressive activity. A component of this aggressive desire for mastery is his competitiveness with other boys. He wishes to be as good or better than they are, to make his mastery known to the outside world.

In the mental sphere, too, this basic aggressiveness is clearly displayed. His chief passion is in mastering the outward environment that surrounds him, in, to use a phrase from football, "throwing it for a loss." This desire leads him to become a scientist, to control-through-knowing some aspect of the world or even of the universe. Or it leads him to become a businessman, wresting a living from the competitive market place. Or it may lead him to become a philosopher, aggressively probing the "why" of the world. Whatever role he plays in life, he must use his aggression to master the environment he selects as his province.

Because of this basic thrusting aggression which largely defines his role in life, a boy is generally given a larger amount of freedom than a girl is. One reason for this is that the male role in life will demand a great deal of self-reliance in the individual, and this has been recognized by society. Men need the protection of the childhood home for a much less protracted period than women do.

In contrast to men, women have a much smaller store of

aggression directed toward the outside world. Their activity is largely directed inward. Psychologically speaking, woman is, in a very real sense, conditioned by her final biological function. At the very center of her nature she is preparing herself for motherhood, and this fact determines the main direction of her psychic energy. Her childhood interests show this clearly. She plays with dolls, she plays house, loves to be around Mother, fantasies marriage, is enormously curious about all of her internal functions. She has, of course, a certain store of interest and aggression which she *can* direct outward, but this characteristic becomes very secondary to her when inward or outward circumstances do not force her to use it.

Intellectually woman is also basically inward. Her most potent faculty is her great intuition, her almost magical ability to understand another person by consulting her own inward nature. This is contrasted to man's objective "intellectual" type of understanding.

In describing the essential characterological structure of the male and contrasting it with the female I am describing absolute types, not people as they are. In actuality most men have a certain store of passivity, of inwardness; and normal women have a certain amount of aggression. However, the normal male will be preponderantly outgoing and aggressive; the normal female's psychic energies will be preponderantly directed inward.

As a direct or indirect result of man's aggression and his commitment to the outside world, in maturity he develops certain behavioristic patterns that are diametrically opposite to female characteristics. Inevitably the frigid woman will use his attributes to show that her man has no interest in her or is weak or is withdrawn or is cruel and wishes to exploit her. Having no objectivity about men she will find in his differences from her further cause for estrangement, fear, and hostility.

Let me give some instances of these behavioristic differences in everyday life.

To the woman, the bearer of children and the nest-maker, the home and everything in it are all-important. She invests her home with a great deal of pride. She loves clean sinks, clean windows, clean floors. She wants things in her nest to be neat and orderly; she has made them that way and she wants them to stay that way.

It will be very easy for her to misunderstand the fact that her husband has invested a major portion of his pride elsewhere: in his work, in his achievements in the outside world.

The cleanliness and neatness of his home he takes for granted. He may even be, by his wife's standards, seemingly antagonistic to neatness, actually sloppy, throwing his clothes around, leaving the sink cluttered, forgetting to use the ash tray, and what not. These things, of course, are not in themselves pleasant traits, but the frigid woman will generalize about them, use them to indicate her man's essential indifference to her.

He may also not notice a new rug or even a new chair in the house. He may have very small patience with any household duties he is forced to undertake: replacing a broken step or even a burned-out bulb. These attitudes can be quite confusing to a woman, and if she has any motive to do so she can easily interpret this kind of male behavior as further evidence of her husband's indifference to her and to the family. It is not; when it occurs it is just male. It may be helpful to her to try to imagine how long her interest in the details of his business life actually hold her attention. The house is her business, and it is not surprising that he behaves the way he does in it, nor is it indicative of any lack of love in him.

Another aspect of man that can be easily misinterpreted is the fact that the male tends to be more sociable, likes to seek out and find a vigorous and sometimes quite varied social life. This, too, is part of his aggressive nature. A woman, though she may be quite gregarious, is generally more content to sit at home, and her immediate circle of friends is enough for her. The frigid woman may try to make much of her husband's aggressive sociability. She is not enough for him; he is restless and dissatisfied, etc.

The vigor and aggressiveness of a man during the course of a social evening are also often misunderstood by women. He may on occasions be quiet, but he sometimes wants to do a great deal of the talking, may even, in his enthusiasm, raise his voice in a conversation. His competitiveness may even embroil him in an actual argument, perhaps a violent one. The woman likes things to run smoothly, to be utterly friendly and tranquil. Her husband's normal social aggressiveness can appear to be rude and crude to her. It can frighten her. Afterward she may confront him with it, accusing him of strutting, of showing off, of cock-of-the-walk behavior. She is merely confronting him with his maleness again.

A very odd difference between men and women is the difference in their reactions to pain and fatigue. Women have a very high threshold for both, and most men have a relatively low one. If a woman gets a burn on her hand she can stick it in butter or in cold water and go on making the dinner. A man with the same burn could be completely incapacitated for a while—and awfully angry at himself besides. The same is true of all sorts of minor aches and illnesses that occur in the normal course of events. Because of this difference in pain thresholds, men tend to pamper themselves or want to be pampered when they have head colds, headaches, sore throats, or other minor illnesses that a woman might ignore. The frigid woman, of course, finds this difference a rich mine to work. She can and does use it to taunt her husband with his "weakness," again showing her essential ignorance of and lack of sympathy with the male nature.

Of course sex itself remains one of the most fruitful sources for resentment and misunderstanding in the frigid woman. Here male aggression can be most clearly seen. The man is stimulated easily by things that would not excite his woman in the least. He is susceptible erotically to all sorts of sights, sounds, and odors. His wife undressing may excite him; her perfume may excite him; he may become aroused if she is looking wan or looking bright-eyed. The frigid woman, not comprehending male reactions or their plural causes, generally feels that his lust is unselective and impersonal. She takes his ardor as an affront for that reason.

In the sexual act the aggressive thrusting of the penis offends too. As passion increases during the act, the strength of the thrust increases, sometimes becomes quite a formidable series of pushes (one of the slang expressions men use for intercourse is "a bang"). This sometimes violent thrusting is a perfectly normal aspect of male sexuality and to the normal woman is of course highly desirable. Frigid women are frightened of it, experience it as an invasion of their integrity, an act of hostility against them.

Nothing could be farther from the fact. In his aggressive movements a man is showing his love in his particular way, his passionate need to lose his isolation, to rid himself of it, to join with his beloved. To misunderstand this is to misunderstand all.

Doubtlessly we could make a longer list of the characteristic things men do and feel that anger or are misunderstood by women with a frigidity problem. If you have started the form of self-inquiry I have advocated you have made your own list and have felt strong negative emotions about many of the items on it.

But the point I wish to emphasize now is that the majority of these negative emotions is caused directly or indirectly by man's underlying and most distinguishing characteristic—his aggression. It is this trait that most clearly defines him, and it is this trait that is at the root of the frigid woman's anger, fear of, and feeling of rejection by men.

She is antagonistic to this aggression because she does not understand it. Since she cannot understand or accept her own role, her feminine nature, she feels that male aggression is opposed to her and she takes every opportunity to prove to herself that this is so. His strength, his ability to master the outside environment make her feel personally nullified, a drab, a slavey. She endlessly contrasts his essential quality of aggression with woman's essential traits, to her detriment.

Now if men *were* out to enslave them, women would be very justified in fearing, hating, envying man's central strength, his aggressiveness. But is he?

A re-examination of this single point can put the whole basic attitude of the frigid woman (once she has allowed herself to feel the negative power of her emotions) back into proper perspective, to correct her fundamental distortion of view. We can do this by looking at the single most important thing men do with their aggression in our society.

"All men have nightmares."

I heard a fellow psychiatrist say those words during an impromptu discussion of male psychology recently, and the phrase struck me as dramatically true. For the majority of men, when they come of age and marry, take on an enormous burden which they may not lay down with any conscience this side of the grave. Quietly and without histrionics they put aside, in the name of love, most of their vaunted freedom and contract to take upon their shoulders full social and economic responsibility for their wives and children.

As a woman, consider for a moment how you would feel if your child should be deprived of the good things of life: proper housing, clothing, education. Consider how you would feel if he should go hungry. Perhaps such ideas have occurred to you and have given you a bad turn momentarily. But they are passing thoughts; a woman does not give them much credence; they are not her direct responsibility; certainly she does not worry about them for long.

But such thoughts, conscious or unconscious, are her husband's daily fare. He knows, and he takes the carking thought to work with him each morning (and every morning) and to bed with him at night, that upon the success or failure of his efforts rest the happiness, health, indeed the very lives of his wife and children. In the ultimate sense he alone must take the full responsibility for them.

I do not think it is possible to exaggerate how seriously men take this responsibility; how much they worry about it. Women, unless they are very close to their men, rarely know how heavily the burden weighs sometimes, for men talk about it but little. They do not want their loved ones to worry.

Men have been shouldering the entire responsibility for their family group since earliest times. I often think, however, when I see the stresses and strains of today's market place, that civilized man has much harder going, psychologically speaking, than his primitive forefathers.

In the first place, the competition creates a terrible strain on the individual male. This competition is not only for preferment and advancement. It is often for his very job itself. Every man knows that if he falters, lets up his ceaseless drive, he can and will be easily replaced.

No level of employment is really free of this endless pressure. The executive must meet and exceed his last year's quota or the quota of his competitors. Those under him must see that he does it, and he scrutinizes their performances most severely and therefore constantly.

Professional men—doctors, lawyers, professors—are under no less pressure for the most part. If the lawyer is self-employed he must constantly seek new clients; if he works for an organization he must exert himself endlessly to avoid being superseded by ambitious peers or by pushing young particles just out of law school and filled with the raw energy of youth. A score of unhappy contingencies can ruin or seriously threaten a doctor's practice, not the least of which is a possible breakdown in his ability to practice. A teacher must work long hours on publishable projects outside of his arduous teaching assignments if he is to advance or even hold his ground.

There is no field of endeavor that a man may enter where he can count on complete economic safety; competition, the need for unremitting year-in, year-out performance, is his life lot. Over all this he knows, too, stands a separate specter upon which he can exert only the remotest control. It is the joblessness which may be caused by the cyclical depressions and recessions that characterize our economy.

It is true; all men have nightmares.

Few if any women could take the kind of daily strain and worry men commit themselves to when they sign the marriage contract. And no woman in her right mind would want to take it. It is true that many women go into the market place, but most of them are waiting only for the day that they marry, or they are already married. Those who stay of their own free will are few and far between, and in my experience some have proven to be difficult people in their family relationships, though some of them are talented. Women are designed for duties different from those of the market place, another kind of stress entirely, and lose or tend to lose their essential womanliness if they stay by choice.

As women look at man's characteristic of aggressiveness in terms of the tremendous duties, daily struggles, and awful responsibilities men must and do assume, they can begin to call up in themselves a different emotion from anger or envy. They can begin to see how altogether worthy of their highest admiration man is. Not just some abstract man, either; the man they love, the man they have married, the man upon whom they have been heaping their criticism, their jealousy and rage.

Far from seeking to enslave our sex, to exploit us through his strength and his aggression, man has put these two great and basic attributes entirely at our service. It is (and always has been) this fact that makes it safe for us to be women, to bear his children with a sense of security, to rear them, knowing that he is there, always and forever, earning our bread, watching over us ceaselessly, keeping his terrible anxieties about us and our safety to himself so that we will not worry as he does.

Certain it is that boys are generally given their freedom a lot earlier than girls. And it is also true that the quality of aggression in the male makes him the wooer and the woman the wooed. I have yet to hear a woman suffering from a frigidity problem who did not deeply resent both of these facts.

But now, looking at the end to which male aggression is directed when it matures, can any woman honestly hold onto such resentment? When she realizes that society instinctively grants him more and earlier freedom so that he may develop the great self-reliance necessary to take on the responsibilities of a family, she cannot validly hold this view any longer.

Nor can she hold onto her resentment of the fact that it is generally the male who initiates the sexual act. For it is the same male aggression which protects her, allows her to be wife and mother, that makes him the wooer and she the wooed. Again, knowing how easily women are distracted from sexual feeling by trivial upsets, by the small things that occur during the day, imagine what would happen if women had to take the male's anxieties and yet be responsible for initiating sex at night. Should such a reversal of roles ever happen to mankind, the world would soon be depopulated. Women must learn to thank God daily for the enormous energy and drive of their men.

In terms of this lifelong commitment of man to the service of his wife and family, let us take another look at the things in his conduct which irritate women, or at least irritate women with a frigidity problem, for now they begin to be understandable. Minor irritabilities, cock-of-the-walk behavior, slackness, sloppiness, whatever—these are either the outlets or the results of the accumulated tensions of a man's day. He will not tell you of the humiliations or defeats or worries of his day in any direct manner usually. As his wife, you must understand that these are the only remonstrances against his hard and anxious struggle that he will permit himself. If you see his behavior in this light it will be difficult to harbor any deep-seated resentment against him; one can only wish to comfort him, to help in any conceivable way to make his burden less onerous, his worries less sharp, his nightmares less frequent.

The espousal of this view of the male, the accurate one, can be another great forward step toward femininity. Seeing her man's aggression in its true light, aimed first and foremost at procuring her safety, happiness, and security, she can now dare to take down, one by one, the precarious defenses she has maintained against him from the beginning of their relationship. She sees that her husband's wonderful aggression actually defines her true role, makes it ever clearer and more desirable to her.

Let us now see how her altered attitude can ultimately affect her and what she can do to hasten and further the process of change.

Chapter 16

THE NATURE OF SURRENDER

When the frigid woman, using the methods described in this section, has divested herself of the destructive fears and false convictions that have been left over from her childhood; and when, in all honesty, she is able to view her husband with new eyes, knowing him to be the hard-beset but loving human being he is rather than an abstract power she had conjured up in his image—when these things are achieved, a profound change begins to take place within her.

This change is not a direct product of her conscious will. Forces which have the character of a tide suddenly freed of long-standing barricades now begin to move irresistibly within her. She feels a new potentiality inside, intimations of an emotional richness she had not dared dream of.

When such a process is loosed within a woman, we say that she is ready to surrender; that, indeed, surrender has already started within her. What does this mean?

It means, in the broadest sense, that at long last she is prepared to become a woman. It means that she is ready, indeed anxious, to yield to her biological and psychological destiny. She has ceased to fear her real role, mentally, spiritually, and physically; ceased to resist it and ceased to resent it. Now she is ready to glory in it. She is ready to love.

When a woman is ready for this final step she no longer needs any urging, any coaxing or coaching. Since this ultimate surrender to her true nature is so natural to a woman, she is often not entirely conscious of its varied manifestations. It is slow, cellular, tidal, certainly unsubject to the conscious will.

Though change is now largely going on outside one's awareness, I should like to emphasize, however, that this phase is very much a part of the *process* that was initiated with the first two steps—of airing one's emotions and fantasies and of revaluating one's husband. We have found that, for a woman whose whole mind and body are, for the first time, taking the path nature intended, it is wise to be as conscious as possible of the process that is going on within her. Many of the feelings are new and powerful and run counter to much of what she has experienced and believed in before. New convictions, new insights, new prospects open up before her. This novel proliferation may be confusing or even frightening. Therefore, the more she understands the nature of her brave new inner world, the more thoroughly and swiftly can she claim it for her own.

For this reason I should like to urge that those who are trying the techniques advocated here continue with the regular daily sessions I mentioned at the beginning. At this point much of the mental activity in such sessions with oneself will be a simple matter of *watching*—of watching the process unfold in oneself, even of celebrating these advances of the unconscious.

In this role of constant observer, however, the conscious mind can also be ready for more aggressive activity. Any tendencies of the old pattern to reassert itself, for angers, fears, fantasies to come out in new guises, can thus be noted and dispensed with before any real damage can be done. Such pullbacks are not only possible but usual, and it is well not to abandon the sessions with oneself until they have disappeared entirely—or as entirely as they're going to.

The process of inner growth that follows when a woman is ready to surrender to her real nature, we have found, traces a rather clear pattern. Some of the new feelings overlap, but mostly they emerge in a given order, each unfolding separately but related to the other as petals to a bud. Let us take them in the usual order of their coming.

As the woman who has suffered from frigidity explodes her groundless fears one by one and explores a new attitude toward men, toward love, toward motherhood, feels a new esteem for her husband—as all these things happen, her life-long *restlessness* begins to depart. For the first time she realizes just *how* restless she has been, how unsatisfied; she feels how precariously balanced her life, inwardly and outwardly, has always felt. Now something deep within her relaxes, lets down. When this happens she is beginning to experience the essential attribute of all that is truly feminine, spiritual tranquillity.

The arrival of this tranquillity, or even the arrival of intimations of it, results from the fact that she is really allowing herself to trust her husband in a very deep sense. It means that she finally realizes that she no longer has to fear or to oppose his strength, but that she can now rely on it to protect her, to give her the secure climate necessary for the full flowering of her femininity.

Feminine tranquillity of spirit is a grace and a beauty of the first order. It is the psychological cornerstone of the happy family. Based on an abiding faith in the goodness and loyalty of her husband, it emanates from a woman who has found herself and pervades those about her, giving them unity and strength. The children of such a mother are strong against the neurotic restlessness of these difficult times. The husband of a wife who has achieved such tranquillity returns from his work to his home as to an oasis, redoubles his loving efforts to make her ever more secure.

Because she can trust no man, the frigid woman's approach to the tasks of life has a difficult, painful, frenetic quality. She feels responsible for everything; guiltily responsible. Details and trivia overwhelm her. She has no unity and has to fight herself, her resentment, her self-rejection to get the simplest things done—her household work, planning the dinner, carrying and fetching the children. Everything *looms*.

With the development of the new quality of tranquillity those details of life that once seemed so difficult become simple. And because they are feminine tasks, household work, planning or getting dinners, keeping the children busy or in line—whatever life demands—soon lose their irksome and irritating quality and become easy, even joyful.

As tranquillity moves over to serenity, becomes more and more a part of her psychic character, a woman begins to realize what a miraculous and wonderful thing womanhood is. Most frequently this realization is ushered in by a sudden awareness of the miracle that her body is able to perform: the miracle of childbirth.

In her frightened heart the frigid woman has always detested and feared her capacity to become pregnant. To her this faculty has seemed onerous and burdensome, a curse. In pregnancy she feels trapped, sick at heart and in body during it, increasingly frightened of delivery as the day of confinement approaches. She views all this as woman's burden;

men, those enviable creatures, are free of such a frightening duty. Indeed, has she not heard that men use pregnancy as a technique of keeping women subject to them! Thus she frets and rages and trembles, rejecting her destiny.

But with her new evaluation of her husband, the deepening of her sense of security, and the growth of her tranquillity, all this childish frightened protest against the miracle of motherhood washes away. Now the scales really fall from her eyes and she feels the full meaning and majesty of what it means to be a woman.

What a privilege it is, she realizes, to be the carrier of the race, the agent of its immortality. What fate could be richer, more beautiful, more filled with wonder and with awe.

I am not exaggerating the importance of this realization. Pride in it, joy in it are the very most central characteristics of the feminine woman. To me its highest expression is in the Madonna paintings which the great Renaissance artists took, over and over again, as a major subject. The Alba Madonna by Raphael catches the essential quality of femininity, expresses it for all to see—and to revere.

Now, with this realization, the last vestiges of her envy of the male and of his role in life disappear. How, she may wonder, with this marvelous capability of hers, inimitable by man, could she ever have depreciated the role of woman, wanted what men have?

At this juncture, or closely following on it, a woman begins to feel her full power, the power that comes to her for her surrender to her destiny. She now realizes that, far from being in a weak position in relationship to man, her position is so strong that she must be careful not to exploit it. One of the deepest and strongest psychological needs of man is his poignant desire for immortality through his children. She could deny him this, or she could make his life miserable while granting him it. Or she can make it the most beautiful and meaningful thing in her life and in his.

What this new realization means to a woman was stated very beautifully in a letter I received from a former patient. We had been able to work only two weeks on her problem, for she came from a different section of the country and could spend only that amount of time in New York City. We worked quickly, and she had been able to surface the hostilities to and misapprehensions about men that had plagued her grown-up life. I had been able also to give her a thumbnail sketch of the problems and changes she might encounter within herself in the future—much as I have described them here. Within six months I had a letter from her. It described the step-by-step process I have depicted: the change in her feelings toward her husband, the incredibly swift growth within her of the new and wonderful serenity. And then she had come to the point where she realized with her whole emotional being the miraculous nature of the female body and the feeling of power and glory that it gave her.

But [she wrote] this feeling of power was quickly followed by an intense feeling of humility. I thought of how I held within me, within my body, the power to bring him the greatest of joys; or to deprive him of it. And then I realized the terrible thing it would be to ever misuse this power. And now I felt really for the first time, despite my former lip service to the idea, the reason why marriage must be considered sacramental. The relationship between husband and wife which results in the unsolvable mystery of birth goes far beyond human understanding. To participate in this mystery really requires a consecration by both. Any lesser attitude toward it is like the laughter of mockery in a holy place.

With this kind of acceptance of her central role, changes now come rapidly to a woman. As she feels the unity of need and goal between her husband and herself, any remaining contentiousness leaves her. In the marriage, consensus now becomes her aim. She is no longer afraid of losing an argument, fearful that she will be forced to do something that is repugnant or humiliating to her, for she realizes that to her husband her welfare is the dearest of all things. And, conversely, his happiness and peace of mind become her first desire.

And now she has tapped in on the greatest psychological joy of woman—her capacity to give. If you remember, in an earlier chapter we called this "essential female altruism," a characteristic rooted in every woman's biological nature. Women who are really secure within themselves and in their roles have an inexhaustible store of this altruism. Frigid women fear this basic characteristic, feeling as they do that men will exploit and abuse their desire to give.

As she reaps the rewards of her new capacity to give of herself unstintingly and fearlessly to her husband and her children, the very appearance of a woman often begins to change. Drawn expressions relax, anxious forehead wrinkles disappear, thin-lipped mouths soften. Indeed, her whole body rounds and softens, taking on the look associated with a tender and giving femininity.

Physical difficulties often disappear. I have known women who had been plagued with intense pre-menstrual and menstrual pains all their lives to lose such symptoms in a matter of weeks. I have known women whose irregular periods have become regularized. And I have also known women with one or two desperately difficult pregnancies behind them who, becoming pregnant again, went through the entire nine months not only without discomfort but with a highly accelerated feeling of pleasure and well-being.

These, then, are the results, or some of them, that a woman who is willing to give up the things of childhood and yield to her true self may expect. The return on such an investment of self is enormous. It is paid in the coinage of love returned for love given; love from one's husband and children, love from friends, new and old, attracted by the endless largesse of the woman who has surrendered all to find all.

Chapter 17

SEXUAL SURRENDER

The ability to achieve normal orgasm can be called the physical counterpart of psychological surrender. In most cases of true frigidity it follows on a woman's surrender of her rebellious and infantile attitudes as the day the night. It is the sign that she has given up the last vestige of resistance to her nature and has embraced womanhood with soul *and* body.

The achievement of orgasm, usually, is the *last* step in the process of growing up. If one reviews in one's mind the actual orgastic experience it is not difficult to see why this is so.

For a woman orgasm requires a trust in one's partner that is absolute. Recall for a moment that the physical experience is often so profound that it entails the loss of consciousness for a period of time. As we know, in sexual intercourse, as in life, man is the actor, woman the passive one, the receiver, the acted upon. Giving oneself up in this passive manner to another human being, making oneself his willing partner to such seismic physical experiences, means one must have complete faith in the other person. In the sexual embrace any trace of buried hostility, fear of one's role, will show clearly and unmistakably.

But there is even more to the psychic state necessary for orgasm than faith in one's partner and readiness to surrender. There must be a sensual eagerness to surrender; in the woman's orgasm *the excitement comes from the act of sur-*

render. There is a tremendous surging physical ecstasy in the yielding itself, in the feeling of being the passive instrument of another person, of being stretched out supinely beneath him, taken up will-lessly by his passion as leaves are swept up before a wind.

There can, it is clear, be no crossed fingers about such yielding, no reservations in such surrender. As one thinks of it one can certainly feel why, of all the steps in the process of yielding, of surrendering, the orgasm should be last. To those who are moving toward it the experience often remains for a time elusive because its very totality, its uncompromising demand that the whole being be swept up in the experience, remains somewhat frightening.

Orgasm, as I have said, is the physical aspect of surrendering. However, while there are similarities between the physical and the psychological experience, there is also an important difference between the two.

The difference is that orgasm cannot be sought entirely rationally. It will arrive when it will arrive, as the end process of a total change in a frigid woman's deepest psychological attitudes. It cannot be sought separately or as an end in itself. Indeed, to seek it directly, to wait upon it, to try to force it are the surest possible ways of postponing its arrival.

The idea that orgasm can be forced is typical of the thinking of a frigid woman. We have seen that, because she is basically frightened, basically mistrusts her husband's love of her and her own femininity, she has to feel that she is "in control" all the time. The trouble with that standpoint is that in real orgasm a woman must be out of control; must willfully, delightedly desire to be entirely so.

The delusion that the orgasm can or should be sought as an end in itself and not as the result of a deep inner change of the kind discussed in the preceding chapters of this section has been fostered by many of the books which have dealt with the problem of frigidity or with the role or responsibility of woman in marriage. One recent book counseled the conscious contraction of certain muscles during intercourse, holding that this would heighten sexual pleasure. Other books emphasize the importance of position during intercourse. Their tacit or stated contention is that orgastic potency can be achieved by mechanical means.

The simple fact is that concentrating on one's sensations during intercourse, wondering if one is feeling the "right" feeling, can destroy real sexual passion more completely than any technique I can think of. We know this from scores of patients. Such a clinical and objective attitude toward local sexual sensations merely reflects the frigid woman's need to be in control of a situation and her fear of surrendering herself to her man. She can get little more from this obsessive scrutiny of her sexual reactions than an even more frustrating experience than usual.

Is there, then, an attitude one can take toward orgasm before one has achieved it? Yes, there is, and we have found it a helpful and productive one. This attitude may be summarized in this fashion: If one has truly pursued the goal of self-surrender, uprooting and exposing attitudes left over from childhood and youth, the ability to achieve orgasm must inevitably arrive. Until that time, and particularly during intercourse, *one must put the matter out of one's mind entirely*.

The growth of a woman's ability to have orgasm is a natural growth. It has been impeded by her psychic attitudes; it resumes its development when these attitudes change. It is as natural a move as the move from winter to spring. Gradually she finds herself allowing her new tenderness and concern for her husband to become a part of the meaning of her sexual embrace. She sees and feels the pleasure her sexual thawing brings him, and this process becomes circular, his increased pleasure giving her more pleasure. And with his pleasure in mind she now seeks out more and more those things that please him, and her exploration leads inevitably to the discovery that what pleases him most, outside of his own sensations, is her pleasure. This mutual spiraling of feeling ultimately climaxes in her unconscious decision to give him the greatest psychological pleasure of all, her total surrender to the delights he can bring her.

For many women the ability to surrender physically comes rather swiftly; to others it is a very gradual process, as though the unconscious mind needed to build up a reserve of reassurances before it felt perfectly secure. In either case, but particularly in the latter, they can be forewarned of one important thing: sexual thaw will not proceed uninterruptedly; there is no straight line from frigidity to true womanhood. I should like to explain this more fully.

When, in the sexual embrace, a woman allows herself to experience more pleasure as her physical sensations increase, a part of her unconscious mind very frequently takes alarm and causes her to draw back from any further immediate advance.

If you stop to ponder this point you will find it readily understandable in terms of our former discussions. The experiences and relationships upon which frigidity is based took place a long time ago, often in very early childhood. They occasioned fear in the child, fear of sexuality, of surrender to one's sensual impulses, or powerful guilt. Now, as one starts to move toward a resumption of one's sensuality, it is almost certain that these irrational, buried fears will try to reassert themselves.

In most cases it is not necessary to uncover the childhood incidents upon which these fears were based. If one will insist on pursuing the techniques for inner change I have described here, these fears will finally become inoperative in the sexual area. It is, however, necessary to know that you *are* experiencing such fears. Generally speaking, they do not show themselves directly. A woman will not say to herself: "That new sensual experience I had last night is causing me alarm."

The fear separates itself from the sensual experience and expresses itself indirectly. The woman may find herself once again becoming quarrelsome, critical of her husband; old feelings of deprivation or of inferiority may reassert themselves with apparently new vigor. And the new sensual capacity may retire once more from view. The reason: the old defenses are protecting one against the new femininity.

Such anxiety reactions, I wish to make clear, should not give any real cause for concern. Indeed, one does not have to analyze them or to investigate them. One merely has to be *aware* that they *are* the result of the new advance in sensuality, the new ability to surrender oneself a bit more completely than formerly. Advance of this kind is never lost in any final sense.

Let me give you an example of a typical reaction to such an advance. The patient was of the type I call the clitoridal woman. Her orgasm had been exclusively clitoral. Together we had covered the ground that I have presented in this section. She had been able to air her feelings about men and about woman's lot; she had corrected her view of men and, in a very real way, had begun to view her husband with the eyes of a loving woman. Then one day she came to me in great excitement. It was unmistakable, she told me; during last night's love-making she had felt, for the first time in her life, distinctly pleasurable vaginal sensations.

But in the next session her attitude was entirely different. She had had a quarrel with her husband over some trivial matter, and she forthwith launched into the kind of tirade against men I had not heard from her for several sessions.

After letting her air her feelings, I pointed out to her the possible connection between her new sensual experience and her regression to her old defenses. She was incredulous and remained so until, a week later, the episode repeated itself in its entirety: vaginal sensations and delight, followed quickly by a quarrel and ill feelings toward her husband. Forewarned, she was now on guard for such negative reactions, and when they did appear, knowing their significance, she was able to handle them, prevent herself from actually acting out her irritational feelings by quarreling with her husband.

In making the above point I do not wish to be misunderstood or thought to be contradicting myself. I am not advising women to fixate obsessively on their new sexual sensations. However, noticing such new experiences will be unavoidable, and I am simply saying that it is helpful to know that they may be followed by minor neurotic regressions.

The above observations now lead me to a closely related matter which I consider to be of central importance.

In the move toward womanhood there comes a juncture in most cases which can be called "the danger point." When a woman is working with a therapist on her problem, the danger when she reaches this point is minimized by the fact that her therapist is aware of the problem and can usually help her to handle it when it arises. If a woman is working on her problem by herself, however, she should be strongly forewarned of her potential reaction.

This danger point generally comes when a woman who has suffered from frigidity has at last allowed herself to experience orgasm for the first time. Her immediate reaction is one of tremendous relief. But this is almost always followed by the same kind of regression I have described above; only this time the pull-back from her own advance and from her husband is far more powerful. We have seen in some of the case histories in the last section just how dangerous this period can be to the entire relationship. Indeed, the wife may at this point precipitate a crisis of such severity that the marriage itself is endangered.

The form the difficulty takes is always individual; it is usually an exaggerated version of the particular woman's most typical neurotic characteristic. If she is argumentative, she is apt to start a fight of proportions heretofore undreamed of. If her tendency is to become depressed, her melancholy can become very, very profound indeed. If she is critical and carping, she can make Craig's wife appear to be a normal, healthy woman.

I am not exaggerating. It is not impossible that many

divorces are caused by wives who, by the natural reassurance that marriage to a tender husband often brings, have moved close to their true natures all unwittingly. They achieve orgasm; and then, without the benefit of any insight, the intense anxiety reaction sets in, causing a powerful desire to flee from the frightening situation.

The pull-back, of course, is caused by an exacerbation of early fears brought on by the orgasmic experience. But again I must emphasize that the chief danger during this period of reaction lies in the fact that the woman sees no connection between her emotional upset and the successful sexual experience she has just achieved. Why should she see such a connection? Orgasm is what she has been consciously waiting for, has it not? It would only be surprising if she did see a connection between the two experiences.

Her emotional outburst represents, at this point, an inner panic. Consider this: in the course of growing up it took her years to construct a defensive system against a feminine sensuality which she had learned was dangerous or wicked. Though this defensive system (her frigidity, her psychological rejection of men, etc.) had deprived her of much, it had at least allowed her to feel secure in some deep manner; she has maintained her defenses in order to hold onto her feeling of unconscious security.

And now, with orgasm, she feels all these defenses swept away in a moment. She feels exposed, guilty, naked to her imaginary enemy, tempted to surrender to him completely. In her panic she forgets the advance she has been making, the revaluation of her attitude toward men, children, womanhood.

She cannot admit the irrational nature of her unconscious fear, even to herself, so she represses it and creates an exterior diversion. Real trouble is always an excellent defense against insight.

In the case histories I have given of frigid women you will recall that the discovery of true feminine sexuality within her often brought a woman to therapy. In a sense the therapist, at the beginning, represents a safe harbor, a protection against the woman's frightening femininity. Coming for help is, in part, a kind of flight in itself; a search for a place to hide.

When women do not understand the nature of their actions in such cases, the flight can take a potentially harmful direction. I have known some who "fall in love" with another man at this juncture. Others feel that they have really discovered just how incompatible their husbands are and think seriously of divorce. Still others develop somatic difficulties, sometimes serious ones. I know two women who had had tuberculosis during adolescence and who both broke down again during this "danger point." In both cases their disease had been considered totally arrested.

I realize, of course, that such reactions sound alarming to a reader. However, my intention in stating the facts here is not to frighten but to forewarn. There is nothing in *reality* to be alarmed about. Feelings are not reality. But a woman must be certain that she does not act upon her feelings. The only danger is that she might.

But, I am often asked, how can one cope with such fears, fears so deep one does not even dare to let them into the conscious mind? The answer is that, generally speaking, you do not have to cope with them in any active way. They will pass. All you have to do is to sit tight, so to speak. The unconscious will in fairly short order (a week, a month) calm down.

Reality, a good reality, can prove to the infantile unconscious that it has nothing to fear. When one has quieted again, resumed the straight line of progress one had been pursuing, orgasm will occur again. This time the reaction of alarm is generally far less. By the third and fourth times it has become virtually nonexistent. The neurotic, defensive portion of one's mind has then been permanently disarmed.

All frigidities are basically related. We could prescribe no general approach that would be helpful if this were not so. However, I have found that there are specific measures that can be of great value if applied to the individual kinds of frigidity. Indeed, if these measures are omitted, the return to full feminine maturity can be slowed down dramatically or even stopped, at least on the sexual level.

I must warn once again, however, that one should be careful to put no reliance on these techniques if they are not combined with the "feeling through" and revaluative processes I have described. With this in mind, then, let us examine these measures that can be taken by individual types.

First let us look at the *masculine type*. As we have seen both in our abstract description and in our case-history approach to this type, the only method of gratification possible for this woman is clitoral. She achieves climax through self-masturbation or through masturbation by her husband. She has few if any vaginal sensations during intercourse, and her orgasmic reactions are confined entirely to the clitoris.

This is so even if she is able to establish contact between her clitoris and her husband's penis in intercourse. In most cases vaginal entrance of the penis is a matter of indifference to such women; to some it is actively disliked.

We have seen how women establish this erotic primacy of the clitoris. Because of early fears connected with becoming women they have firmly rejected the vagina. They have held onto infantile and pubertal masturbation long past the point when it is normal for a girl to give it up.

Now, with a new evaluation of the meaning of feminine sexuality, with a new tenderness and warmth toward their husbands available to them, the time at length comes when it is possible for them to switch from clitoral sensations to vaginal. However, the pathways for satisfaction have been set up for many years, the "habit" of clitoral climax has been deeply established. What should they do?

We have found that, if the clitoridal woman wishes to achieve a more mature form of sexual satisfaction she may be aided in reaching her goal if she can give up the form of gratification she now employs. This form of gratification still symbolizes an attachment to the earlier form of sexuality. For that reason, of course, it is a defense against the type of sexuality that stands for psychic maturity. The simple decision to abandon the less mature form of gratification often signifies a deep decision within a woman: the decision to take the final step toward womanhood.

On the other hand, many women experience the abandonment of clitoral gratification as a keen deprivation and deeply resent it. In such cases the resentment signifies that they have not sufficiently "felt through" their childhood defenses against femininity.

Obviously there are only two possible steps to take: one can continue the practice of masturbation or one can examine the resentment that is caused by giving it up. If a woman decides on the first step, progress toward the goal of vaginal orgasm may be slowed down or halted completely.

If, however, one decides to examine the resentment more closely, using the "feeling through" technique I have described, the bases upon which the resentment rests may be discovered and disposed of, just as resentments against men and against motherhood were disposed of. Indeed, many of the same feelings, though now more specifically related to sexuality, often come out.

Let me give an example. A patient with a clitoridal fixation had worked through many of her negative feelings toward her husband; she had seen that these feelings had been

based on an irrational envy and fear of men and a depreciation of women. Her progress, however, seemed to halt completely when she attempted to give up clitoral masturbation.

All of her early feelings toward men returned, only now
they referred to the act of intercourse. Men were the lucky
ones; they were on top. Just as in life. Woman's classical
sexual position in our civilization (on the bottom) was "degrading and humiliating." It represented her position vis-à-
vis men in life. As in life, men were the ones for whom
irresponsible enjoyment was designed; no wonder they could
enjoy sex so much; and they couldn't get pregnant; they
didn't have to menstruate, etc., etc.

She aired these irrational feelings quite completely and
saw them for what they were. She saw that they were a
recapitulation, in sexual terms, of the negative feelings she
had expressed earlier toward men. She realized, too, that her
feeling that it was humiliating and degrading to be "on the
bottom" really showed her deep distress, fear of, and underlying depression about what she took to be woman's role
in life.

The patient was rather surprised to see these irrational
feelings reappearing. However, because of her earlier work
on her psychological defenses, it was not too difficult for
her to dispose of these negative attitudes toward the sexual
act and to integrate her positive feelings about womanhood
with woman's sexual role. At that point she was not far from
achieving vaginal orgasm. Within a month or so she had
achieved it.

When a woman consciously abandons clitoral gratification
in favor of her search for a deeper and more abiding joy,
the switch from clitoris to vagina usually takes place gradually. I have known cases in which it has happened rather
quickly, but it is more frequently a matter of two, three, or
even more months.

One further word on this type: the clitoridal woman may
discover that she cannot take the final step to vaginal primacy alone. She may need direct and expert counsel. This
should in no way discourage her. The problem is a deep-
seated one, but it almost certainly can be resolved. If after
a few months of trying to handle the problem alone one
finds out that too little progress is being achieved, I strongly
urge that outside help be sought (see Addenda I, pages 190-
191, for methods of obtaining the correct kind of aid).

I have heard the therapy for *total frigidity* described as
"a problem in rerearing." Recalling the case history of Patricia Agnew, one can easily see why this phrase is so apt.

The causes of this kind of frigidity go back to infancy. Punishment for infantile masturbation and/or an overly strong early fixation on the male parent causes the child to repress her sexual feeling entirely. She does not go through, in any complete way, the normal stages of psycho-sexual development; a part of her, the sensual and sexual part, remains frozen in the bud.

In my opinion, psychotherapy is frequently indicated when the frigidity is of this total type. The sexual aspect of the problem is sometimes too deeply seated for the individual to handle alone.

However, I know of several women who, when therapy was not possible, were able to make great strides toward truly feminine values and behavior by adopting the procedures described in this section. Though some of them were not able to achieve orgasm, the psychological change they were able to effect in their personalities added greatly to their general happiness and security in marriage. A few even were able to achieve orgasm.

For women with this form and degree of frigidity who wish to or must attempt to approach their problem without outside aid, I should like to point out that if general sexual development is resumed it will tend to recapitulate the stages of psycho-sexual growth we have described. Thus we find that when such women, through insight, are once again able to experience sensual feeling they sometimes go through a period of self-masturbation. Recall that this stage had been omitted in their development.

I should like to emphasize that, in terms of the final resolution of her sexual frigidity, this masturbation is perfectly normal for this kind of woman—just as it is contraindicated for the masculine or clitoridal woman. The totally frigid woman is making up for phases of development she had missed in growing up. Guilt feelings about masturbation in such cases are harmful, and the ego of the individual can be put in the service of overcoming such emotions. For those who have moral feelings against masturbation it is sometimes helpful to realize that modern scientific findings indicate that societal prohibitions against it were partly based on insufficient and incorrect information. It was believed for centuries that pubertal or infantile masturbation was harmful physically and mentally. It has now been clearly demonstrated, however, that the only harm of any kind that can come from masturbation is the psychological harm that is caused by guilt feelings connected with it.

The fact is that, in attempting to establish her lost sexuality, the totally frigid woman may be helped by encouraging any sensuality, however meager, she may discover in herself, whether it is psychological or physical. The sensuous feelings engendered by sun-bathing, of the press of the earth under one when lying down in a field or under a tree, the soft beauty of the moon on a hazy night, the warmth and coziness of a fireplace as the rain beats upon the roof—if she will allow her body and mind to enjoy these kinds of things, they can help to awaken her dormant sensuality, can help her to move back from her dusty sensationless condition toward a reappreciation of the glory of the senses.

Some women may discover (if they can consciously dispense with their inhibitions or with a hindering sense of propriety) that they are able to experience sensual feelings of a moderately keen nature in areas which are secondarily erotic. During our work together one woman suddenly discovered that she enjoyed having her back stroked by her husband. Another discovered that though she could not enjoy kissing her husband if she was in bed with him she could if she remained fully clothed in the living room. A third was able to respond quite strongly to clitoral stroking if she had a drink of liquor with her husband beforehand. In each case the sensual capacities described in these women preceded their work with me. But it was only when they realized that they possessed unexplored potentialities and that these could be used to enrichen their sensual lives, to move them closer to the ultimate experience of love, did they dare to take their first tentative steps toward maturity.

As we have observed, *partial frigidity* includes those degrees of frigidity that lie between total frigidity and normalcy. This includes such a large range of sexual reaction (or the lack of it) that it would not be possible to describe specific measures that would be helpful in all cases.

However, those who find they are closer to total frigidity on this scale than to normalcy often discover that the general techniques just described are helpful. Many of these, if they persevere, will find that they will ultimately achieve orgasm without requiring psychotherapy. Others, after determining the distance they can go on their own, may wish to seek outside help.

For those who lie closer to normal feminine sexual reactions it is usually sufficient to persist in the techniques for self-discovery and self-realization described earlier in this section.

As we saw when we examined *psychic frigidity,* it seemed to be the exception that proved the rule. Women of this type are able to have orgasms that are apparently normal. But they cannot form a relationship with any man that will endure. They frequently select ineligible men as partners or, if by chance the man happens to become eligible, they will then flee the relationship. If they cannot flee it they become sexually frigid.

We have found that women with this type of frigidity can help themselves by denying themselves the easy gratification to which they are accustomed. Their facile sensuality is a red herring used to disguise their real fears from themselves. They can come to grips with these fears only when they allow themselves to enter a close psychological relationship with an eligible member of the opposite sex.

I have called the steps by which a woman moves from frigidity to emotional and sexual maturity a "process." Once really started, it tends, almost by inertia, to complete itself, needing only a kind of minimal guidance from one's intelligence and a few specific facts.

For the sake of clarity, then, let us review what the steps in this process are.

It is launched by the surfacing of negative emotions and fantasies from which the frigid woman has been hiding. These emotions and fantasies reflect an underlying attitude toward the opposite sex which is based on early childhood fears and misunderstandings and which is seriously affecting one's ability to love. As the emotions are exposed to full view they lose their power for harm, for it is only when they are partially or totally hidden from oneself that their primitive force is dangerous. When they are exposed to the light of intelligence and judgment, their power over one can at first be greatly reduced and finally can be disposed of entirely.

When all or most of one's negative daydreams and emotions have been exposed, step two can be taken. This is a revaluation of the male in terms of his real nature and real goals. We saw that his real nature is basically aggressive, and one of his chief aims in life is to put this aggression to work for his wife and family. Viewed from this standpoint, man's differences from woman are seen in their true light. The frigid woman, from this revaluation, learns that she can now let down her defenses, knowing that her husband, far from being hostile or wishing to enslave or exploit her, is her loving ally. She sees that his once-feared aggression is the very thing that makes it really safe for her to be a woman.

From this realization, on a deep level of her personality,

the next step follows naturally. She first achieves a tranquillity and then a serenity she had not known before. This is followed by an acceptance of and a surrender to her real role—that of a loving and wise wife who glories in her womanly functions and in her man's love.

The last step was seen to be the achievement of orgasm as a natural sequel to her psychological maturation. This part of the process we saw was attended by a resurgence of early anxiety when orgasm finally occurred. This anxiety caused a desire to flee from the newly acquired ability to love. However, the only danger at this juncture was seen to be the possibility that the anxious woman might act upon her fears. Forewarned of this reaction, she is forearmed, and by seeking further insights and waiting out the anxiety she will find that it will gradually subside completely.

These general steps, then, outline the process that can lead to recovery. I can add little to them. I have seen this method work for many women and I know of no other that will.

Patience and faith are the prime requisites for emotional maturation. Nobody can name the time it will take for any given individual to cross the bridge to womanhood. But that most women can cross it, there can be no doubt. Those who have gone before make that point ultimately clear.

Chapter 18

THE ROLE OF THE MALE

When a woman decides to cross the bridge from frigidity to mature femininity her husband's attitudes, feelings, and reactions can be all-important.

I said earlier that we have found that the man is rarely responsible for his wife's frigidity; that it developed long before he met her. However, he must understand that, when she begins to assume responsibility for her difficulty, responsibilities of a new kind are thrust on him too. In the beginning at least, and contrary to what he might expect of himself, he may not like these responsibilities at all. He may find that he has a very negative attitude toward his wife's attempt to mature, that indeed he does not want her to.

It is very necessary for a man to understand the elements that make his role appear to him to be very difficult during such a period. In a sense, if the project is to succeed, he must be as aware of his reactions as his wife is of hers.

What, then, are the main elements of his reactions?

In the first place, the husband of a frigid woman generally has a great store of repressed resentment toward his wife. This is quite understandable, of course. He has been the chief recipient of her very strong negative feelings toward life, people, love, and sex.

As we have seen, the frigid woman has a strong tendency to blame others for her difficulties. Her husband, doubtlessly, has received his full quota of such irrational blame from her. He has also been the main victim of all the other neurotic components of frigidity—the envy and mistrust she has of the entire male sex, the endless complaints she directs against her household duties, her general inability to handle even the trivia of every woman's everyday life with any grace or ease.

In addition to her quarreling and complaints he has had to accept a tremendous amount of emotional frustration. Frigidity does not permit much honest or real interpersonal warmth, and the male has had to do without a normal amount of affection. His sexual frustration, too, is great. We saw in the case of the clitoridal woman just how laborious and boring the act of love can become to the man. It is not necessary to labor the point of how cumulatively bleak sexual intercourse with an unresponding partner can become.

All this (and more) that a man has gone through with a frigid wife must have a very definite effect on him. He builds up attitudes and develops defenses which allow him to preserve his equilibrium within the framework of his marriage as it is.

Some of these defenses are psychological, some external.

The chief psychological defense he uses is a general withdrawal; he pulls back from "caring" about the unhappy circumstances of his married life. He may cease to react, either to his wife's attacks on him or to her general complaints. He may cease, too, to care very much about the failure of their sexual life. His withdrawal from the problem may be marked by actual sexual impotence with his wife. Or he may, in response to his wife's rejection of sex, take a purely mechanical attitude toward intercourse, getting it over with as quickly as possible, taking it like a hurried but necessary meal.

His external defenses against his home life may be a withdrawal from it. He may reorganize his social life around a men's social or athletic club, spending a great deal of time with "the boys." He may take to drinking at bars in the evening, forming a circle of cronies whom he likes to be with. He may do any of a number of things that take him out of his home in the evening and give him substitute pleasures.

Now of course there is nothing the least bit reprehensible about the erection of such defenses if one's marriage and home life are unsatisfactory. Indeed, such defenses may keep a marriage together by allowing the man to get some compensatory pleasures out of life.

One husband said just this in so many words to me recently. "If I hadn't taken a firm stand within myself," he told me, "the marriage would have broken up long ago. I simply decided that, if things were to work out at all, I just had to pull back from her and not take what she said to me seriously. If I went on believing half of the attacks she made on me I couldn't have lived with myself. And since sex was no fun, what was there left between us? I've made up a social life of sorts outside of the family for myself. At least I get a little fun out of life, and since I'm not around mainly I'm not boring her so much and she's not boring me so much."

But the danger is that such defenses and such compensatory activities will be held onto even if the marriage has been given a chance to turn from a meaningless one into a deeply meaningful and joyful one. A husband who wishes to help his wife in her struggle to become a woman, who wishes to make a marriage where only the semblance of one now exists, must now examine his attitudes with great honesty, courage, and thoroughness.

The way ahead of him at the beginning will not be by any means clear or easygoing. The initial progress of his wife as she undertakes to change is often barely perceptible. Why should he have any hope that anything new, exciting, or beautiful could develop from such tentative starts? And what motive can he develop to turn back, emotionally and sexually, to a woman who has so often and so thoroughly rejected and frustrated him? A very strong part of him feels that he has worked out a precarious inner and outer equilibrium which at least keeps this semblance of marriage from falling apart entirely. He generally actively resents the demand on him to alter his attitude, to see his wife through the inner odyssey on which she now wishes to embark.

We have found that at such a juncture a husband is often helped to alter his defensive attitude by seriously reflecting on the picture of marriage and love he had when he first fell in love with his wife. He should then compare that image of a relationship with the custom-staled and defeated feelings he has now, compare his first hopes of creatively shared lives with the empty realities of the present, the time-wasting, essentially loveless activities he now engages in.

Memories and thoughts of this kind can make him angry, the way a *man* can get angry, healthfully and aggressively; not at his wife, who now wants to make up for all that has been lost, but at himself for his passive acceptance and easy adjustment to a defeated life, a life that has become a resigned and pointless existence. Such anger is good because it can clear his inner atmosphere; it can start him back with renewed resolution on the road to his real desires. For no man who feels worthy of his manhood ever really accepts a half existence in love of the kind I have just depicted.

We have found, too, that such husbands can remotivate themselves if they will contemplate the potentialities of womanhood toward which their wives now consciously aspire. I have tried throughout this book to show, in some of their variety, the magnificent and exciting qualities that characterize true womanhood. I have shown how giving women can be in their love, how supportive, how filled with deep warmth and understanding. And I have tried to show how, in sex itself, there is no responsiveness that can compare even remotely with that of a loved and emotionally secure woman. If at this critical point in his marriage a man can clarify what he really wants and then develop the patience to wait for it, he will be most thoroughly rewarded.

Patience is *very* important. He will need all of it he can muster for a time and, at certain points, he may have to remind himself hard of the rewards at the end of the journey. He can, we find, be greatly helped by having as thorough a knowledge as possible of the psychological problems his wife will encounter in her hegira to womanhood.

I have shown that the path to feminine maturity is not a straight one. The traveler will often become frightened of the very progress she is making and for a short time will tend to pull back into her former neurotic defenses. At such a point the husband must be very clear that she has not pulled back for good.

The critical period, as we have seen, in a woman's forward march, the thing that is apt to make her pull back most strongly and with most anxiety, is her first encounter with real orgasm. However, the husband must realize once more that this regression is temporary, too, even though it lasts for several weeks or, in some cases, longer. The solicitude of her husband at this point and the reassurance she gets from the knowledge of his love can be the main factors in her final victory over her difficulty.

Many psychiatrists make it a practice to discuss with husbands, whenever it is feasible, the importance of their role in the complete recovery of their wives. It is a very rare man who, after such discussions, cannot or will not mobilize his resources to aid his wife and to see her through her hard struggle. And I know of no woman who has won a victory over her frigidity who has ignored the fact that her husband's help was decisive.

In addition to changing his defensive attitude toward his

wife (or perhaps searching for and recapturing his earlier feelings toward her), in what other ways can a husband be helpful to his wife as she struggles toward maturity?

I would say that the primary virtue he should cultivate in himself is sensitivity, particularly sensitivity to any advances or changes in her manner of relating to him, to their children, or to friends in their immediate circle. She is trying to rid herself of a lifelong mistrust of men and fear of them. She is trying to dare to be soft, warm, and giving. Every recognition she gets for her efforts will be like manna to her. In many ways she is like a frightened child, and only total acceptance can give her enough courage to advance further.

Let me give a simple example of what I mean: The relationship between a woman patient of mine and her husband had, in the course of their five-year marriage, deteriorated sadly. In their courtship days they had been in the habit of giving each other gifts, frequent and personally meaningful gifts. But now, even on birthdays, they bought presents "for the home" rather than for each other.

During the course of our work the wife, one cold winter day, on the spur of a tender moment, bought her husband a very bright yellow scarf and presented it to him that night. I learned later from him that his first impulse on receiving the gift was to laugh. He dressed most conservatively, and the garish scarf was very much out of keeping with his tastes.

He did not laugh, however, realizing that the gift was an expression of something new in his wife, that it showed a new concern for him and an attempt to begin to show it. Instead he kissed her tenderly and wore the scarf to his office the next day. When he came home that night he presented her with a lovely platinum watch of a make he had once heard her admire. "She looked down for a moment," he told me, "as though she were confused, and then she looked up at me and put her arms around me and wept a very long time." Those tears, of course, were the sure beginning of a deep thaw. His sensitivity to his wife's need at this point in her life had been a decisive element, and her progress from that point on was greatly accelerated.

In counseling husbands to be sensitively attentive to their wives' needs during this period of change I must warn against one thing. Insincerity or artificiality will not work at all, indeed could actually be harmful. Women are deeply intuitive and can detect any hypocritical attempt to manipulate them. It is not wise to try to express love if you do not feel it. A man who cannot experience real feeling toward his wife should put his main effort into self-inquiry. He may discover that the anger and hurt that have built up in him during the unhappy years that are past are too great to handle alone and he may wish to discuss these intransigent feelings with a counselor or psychiatrist.

I know of one man who, paying lip service to the idea of helping his wife, put in a weekly order at the local florist shop for flowers. When in the next three months she had received "enough," as she put it, "for an elaborate funeral," she begged him to stop sending them.

Another man, having ignored any social life with his wife for years, was told that she should get away from her household duties occasionally. He suddenly insisted, therefore, on dragging her on a round of night clubs and theater parties that would have exhausted Elsa Maxwell. His wife was essentially rather shy and withdrawn and of course resented this enforced and artificial approach to her real needs.

Women rightly consider these kinds of gestures a mockery, an expression of a latent hostility toward them rather than as an expression of love. Of course women love luxury, going out, gifts—but only when they express a sensitive awareness on the part of the giver. A rule of thumb that works is to do what one feels but to refrain firmly from doing what one doesn't feel. Somebody once said that the proper mixture for the real lover is 80 per cent male aggression and 20 per cent feminine sensitivity. The formula has much to recommend it.

One important thing that husbands and wives must learn to do is to share their deeper thoughts, problems, and feelings with one another. Over the years the general withdrawal of both partners has made communication of any kind most superficial, and hope of any important contact through conversation has been abandoned almost entirely. When the wife has finally told her husband of her determination to attack her problem frontally, the couple now have a new opportunity for establishing deep lines of communication. If the husband can seize on this new chance, divest himself of his lonely and habitual reticence, he can help his wife and their entire relationship immeasurably.

Everything may be discussed in such conversations, although one should avoid any recrimination or "confessions" that would hurt the other. Conversation about one's emotional or reality difficulties, about one's loneliness, plans, successes, fears, and hopes, are deeply moving to a woman. If a man can learn to share his real inner life with his wife it will help her to realize once more the importance of the woman's role, make her know that she has her husband's confidence in those things that are of real importance to him.

As I have pointed out, frigid women have little knowledge of what men are really like. Basically they see men as "powers," without worries or fears. When they learn from their husbands' own lips their real feelings, these women are very greatly aided in changing their underlying attitudes.

One woman told me that her whole marriage-long conception of her husband had been completely altered by one emotional confession from him. She had told him that she had finally realized her frigidity had been the cause of the problem between them and that she had determined to attempt to change herself. He listened quietly as she talked and was silent for a moment when she finished. Then he said in a low voice: "I have been terribly lonely without you." This honest communication reached past all her neurotic defenses, informed her simply and directly how important her decision was to him, how human and needful the husband she had feared and rejected really was.

It is in such real, such personal exchanges with his wife that a man most often begins to reap the rewards his wife's decision to change will bring him. As he expresses himself more and her security in him deepens, he begins to encounter the depths of tranquillity that have always lain beneath her defensive exterior; he begins to feel her great capacity to give him something that he has missed, missed terribly—a companionship, support, and love that ask for nothing but to be needed. In this way a new and profound mutuality develops and, cleared of the fears that have impeded it, the real marriage between these two people can begin to flourish.

In the sexual aspect of the marriage, as in its psychological aspect, sensitivity is also the key word for the husband who wishes to help his wife.

In every case of frigidity that I have encountered the sexual life between husband and wife has, through the years, become an extremely self-conscious one. The wife generally is acutely aware of every genital sensation that she has or every sensation that she does not have. Her chronic sense of failure is at the root of this hawk-like attention to her reactions. Often this self-concern has been encouraged by reading books that emphasize the mechanical aspects of sexual love, giving her false hopes that somehow she is going to be able to solve her orgastic problem if she can only get in the right position, make the right movement, contract the right muscles at the right time, or teach her husband the right techniques.

Under such circumstances it is impossible for a husband not to react to his wife's hyper-narcissism. He tends then to put his awareness of her experience ahead of his own enjoyment. This is one of the prime reasons why the sex act for both of them has become anxious and dull.

In sex one's body can feel only its own raptures. Even the exquisite sensation of giving the partner pleasure is psychological and, by definition, important only when it heightens one's pleasure, not when it decreases it.

It is very important, therefore, for the husband to drop his self-consciousness about his wife's pleasures or lack of them during intercourse. In fact, both must start with a clean slate on this score, take the healthy natural view that sexual sensation is a self-centered, even selfish, matter basically. Overconcern for the other can rob it of its lusty spontaneity entirely.

This may strike a man as a new conception. In most books on married sexuality the mutuality of the act is the point emphasized; such books always speak glowingly of the pleasure one experiences in the other's reactions. When frigidity is present this "mutuality" can become a mockery.

A woman suffering from frigidity will be very relieved if her husband will make a gentle but blanket announcement to her that she is to drop her entire concern with orgasm until it happens. I have pointed out before that this indeed must be her working attitude before she has her first orgasmic experience. For a husband to affirm that this attitude is also his can be a great reassurance to her. She will then allow herself to really enjoy his "selfish" ecstasy without neurotically fixing on her own localized sensations. Indulging the deeply feminine role of *giving* pleasure can be more exciting to her than any other thing.

Now a word about foreplay—in my opinion one of the most grossly misunderstood words in the language. Many men, and women too, take it to mean solely a duty-bound interval in which a man tries to arouse a woman by physically caressing and kissing her. This mechanistic interpretation is based on the oft-quoted statement that women are slower to respond sexually than men and that it is the man's duty to arouse her.

I think it is absolutely necessary for this particular conception of foreplay to be expanded considerably where women who have had a sexual difficulty are concerned. As we have seen over and over again, frigidity in women is caused by psychological problems of a very specific kind. Any exclusively mechanical approach to these difficulties is foredoomed to failure.

Husbands of women with a frigidity problem are well advised to consider foreplay primarily a psychological rather than a physical matter.

If you will recall the stages of development the growing girl goes through, you will remember that they culminate in adolescence. During that stage a long romantic dream prepares the girl for real love. This dream of romance never leaves a woman. Foreplay is most successful when it arouses these dormant romantic feelings. Woman is truly an incurable romantic.

But what does romance really mean to her? And how can the romantic feeling be conjured up?

Romantic feelings are aroused in a woman when she feels that her husband's entire emotion is fixed on her tenderly and lovingly. She feels romantic when all the other goals and needs and duties of life are for the time being relinquished. In such a situation she dares to relax, to loaf and invite her soul, to concentrate on her deep belief that love is centrally important, the thing that gives life its meaning and its beauty. Every woman, at the heart's deep core, wishes to give all for love.

Such a mood of romance cannot, of course, be trumped up suddenly, nor can it be created by a man who feels cynical or abashed by it. To woo a woman successfully, a man must believe in her dream of love and become a passionate sharer in it.

Certain things that remove a couple for a while from the highly goal-centered activities of daily life help to create this romantic mood. A housewife will respond to a luxurious evening out; putting on an evening gown can separate her from her housekeeping, penny-pinching view of herself, and the sight of her husband in a tuxedo can fill her romantic cup to the brim. A few champagnes and dancing to a good orchestra, and the magic is complete.

Picnics together, too, can engender a deeply romantic feeling in a wife. But of course the children should not be along. And the whole thing should be carried off with a little style. Wine, a good one, is a must, and the man should know beforehand of a fine and very private spot for the picnic.

I have known several women who have broken through the barriers of sexual frigidity during ocean cruises. These seem to represent the romantic circumstance par excellence, and a husband who can afford them should add them to his loving calculations.

In my opinion, husbands and wives should arrange their lives to get some vacation time alone together. With even the best intentions the duties and responsibilities of life close in on one, tend to take some of the bloom off the rose. A week, a month if possible, alone together can help to re-establish vitality and meaning in a marriage.

The fact that a man has stayed with a woman despite her frigidity and the problems it causes is a testament to the abiding love he has for her. If he will forget his old despair now that his wife has taken responsibility in the relationship, call on his real manhood to reassert itself in helping her to her goal, his rewards can be as bounteous as femininity can bestow.

Chapter 19

THE LORE OF LOVE

In this book, as you have noted, I have taken a firm stand against any mechanical approach to love or love-making. This represents the psychiatric view of love and is based on the premise that frigidity is psychological in nature and that the resolution of it must be therefore a psychological one.

The mechanical approach is based on the premise that love-making is an art or even a science that can be learned, as the piano or chemistry can be learned. From the psychiatric view the so-called art of love is instinctual. The perfectly free person, if one can be imagined, would, if he loved and were loved in return, soon become a sophisticated practitioner of this art with the barest of preparation.

I recall an anecdote that illustrates this point. It was told to me by a sociologist who was conducting a survey of married couples in an effort to find the correlation between premarital advice and sexual happiness. While questioning one healthy couple whose marriage was obviously happy, he asked the husband:

"And did your parents give you any advice?"

"Yes."

"Which parent?"

"My father."

"Did he give you a thorough briefing?"

Pause. "Yes, it was brief." Pause. "And it was thorough."

"What did he tell you?"

"You want his words?"

"Yes, if you like."

"He said, 'Everything goes.' "

However, such free spirits as this one are relatively rare in our society. Usually more instruction is needed. Taboos against sexuality have characterized Western civilization. The art of love, therefore, seems to me to be largely the art of getting over societally induced ignorance, superstition, and inhibition.

Here's how I view the matter. When through the methods employed in this section or through therapy one has at length achieved psychological maturity and therefore vaginal orgasm is no longer blocked, an examination of some of the technical information about love-making can be helpful. Before that point, such lore tends to lead to an inhibiting self-consciousness.

It is generally agreed by students of the matter that spontaneity in sexual relations must never be lost. Married life tends to impose a rather rigid pattern in all areas of living. Such routinization is a necessity if the world's work is to get done. For most people, for example, it becomes necessary to breakfast every day at the same time, in the same place, and in the same manner. If one allows this to happen to sexuality one is imprisoning the unicorn, exposing love-making to a loss of its magic.

Variety is the spice that married love often needs, and it takes no great effort to be various in love-making. It takes only a sense of its importance and the knowledge of a few minimal facts.

One method of preserving spontaneity is to prevent love-making from always occurring at the same time. Evenings in most homes tend to follow a pattern. Supper must be cooked, dishes must be done, children must be put to bed. And then there's television or guests. I have had many men and women defend the proposition that, since love-making tends to make them sleepy when it is finished, the last moments of the day are by necessity the time for love.

But this is making convenience a necessity. And love is too beautiful, too centrally important to be domesticated so. If it can laugh at locksmiths, it can also, once every week or two, laugh behind locked bedroom doors. Children have homework to do or a television program to watch, and anyhow, it is good for them to realize that Mother and Father spend some time alone and love to.

Dishes can wait occasionally, too, at least in the name of love. And a television program is rarely so good or demanding that a delicious sleepiness won't improve it.

Desire often arises unbidden and for no apparently rational reason. Men are more subject to outside stimuli than women and are perhaps more uninhibited, so the inception of love-making at unroutine times may most frequently originate with them. But women, too, when they feel the urge should realize that they can initiate a passionate interlude and should not prevent themselves from doing so. It is proper and good that a woman should do this. And her husband will love it.

I am assuming that the partners in such delightfully off-hour trysts are sensitive to each other's responses. What every man and woman must realize is that it is perfectly all right to say no if one is fatigued or preoccupied. But the nay-saying must be gentle, and if it is so and the partner who makes the advance is hurt, he or she must examine the rejected feeling, take full responsibility for it, and dispose of it. Holding onto such feelings causes one to fear making advances and this will deprive the relationship of one of the best techniques for maintaining spontaneity. It is insensitive and unloving to force a partner by sulking or other forms of psychological blackmail to satisfy a need. It is far easier for the ardent one to wait; the time will come soon enough; the fact that you have announced your desire has a delayed reaction on your loved one.

Waking in the middle of the night, many men find themselves prepared for love-making, the penis firmly erect. And many women love to be awakened from their sleep to find themselves mistily, dreamily in the embrace of love; the body on waking is often very sensual.

Changes on the time for love can be rung in a variety of ways, and it is advisable to see that they are. Not too much effort is necessary; the hour at the end of the day when one is preparing for sleep will still remain the basic time for intercourse. It will need but an occasional switch in time to keep this customary trysting hour from losing its quality of ever-renewed excitement.

Another and perhaps even more basic technique for preserving the spontaneity of sex is that of varying the position used during intercourse. In most relationships one preferred position generally evolves. If this position is always adopted, the feeling of a monotonous repetitiveness can enter the love situation, and this must be guarded against.

This fact has been recognized from earliest times, and efforts to combat it have given rise through the centuries to a vast number of books on the subject. Hindu, Greek, Roman, and Persian literature record hundreds of sexual positions and animadversions, and if one has a library of erotica available and is sufficiently curious these positions may be studied. However, such a proliferation of detail can become exhausting and even morbid and absurd—though perhaps gaily absurd. Most of the modern books which dispense direct sexual advice obtain their material from these ancient sources.

There are only five basic positions which have real relevance to most couples. I am going to describe them so that when you encounter them or wish yourself to change from your usual position you will not feel that they are strange, awkward, or so exotic as to cause you feelings of shyness, embarrassment, or guilt.

The first position, of course, is the ventro-ventral (or face to face) position, with the man on top and the woman on the bottom with her knees up. Not even the most puritanically reared person will demur at this position, for it is the classical sexual position used in our society.

It is, if used properly, perhaps the best position for sexual union. It allows for deep penetration of the vagina by the penis, and because it leaves the pelvic regions of both partners free, it allows for variety in sexual movement, though the man has more freedom of movement in this position than the woman.

There's an old but apt joke about this position. A young chorus girl asks an older one what her definition of a gentleman is. The older one promptly replies: "One who leans on his elbows." Men should remember that this fact can be pertinent. The full weight of the heavy man can be quite tiring even to a very passionate woman.

A pleasant variant of this position can be achieved if a pillow is placed under the buttocks of the woman before intercourse. If it is placed a little toward the small of the back, those women who receive preliminary pleasure from friction between the clitoris and the penis will find the contact easier to effect. If it is placed a bit forward it will be very exciting to those who get a great deal of sensation from pressure of the penis against the posterior walls of the vagina.

Generally in this classical position the woman simply spreads her legs and raises them (lying with the legs straight down makes vaginal entrance difficult for the male). Those who enjoy stimulation of the posterior vaginal wall may lock their legs around their partner's hips. Those who in the initial stages of intercourse are most aroused by clitoral stimulation may close their legs; in this position the man is half kneeling, straddling his partner's hips. This latter position is not too comfortable for the man if it is maintained for long. A less arduous position for the man is achieved if he straddles one of his partner's legs and enters the vagina at a slightly oblique angle. This allows the woman to close the leg that is free, which gives maximum contact of all portions of the vulva with the penis.

The next major position reverses the top-bottom roles. The woman, in this variant, is on the top, the man on the bottom.

Many couples feel inhibited about this position. The man will often feel "feminized," the woman "masculinized." Such relativistic concepts of what is male and what is female could actually have any application only if this were the chief position in which a couple had intercourse. And even this fact could be altered by circumstance; for example, the woman might be physically very small and the man very large and heavy.

This position is adopted either as a spontaneous change for variety's sake or because the woman may be feeling far more energetic than the man at the moment; the partner on top, of course, does the major portion of the moving. Psychologically this position can represent an expression of tenderness on the woman's part. If her husband feels sensual but fatigued, she can give him pleasure without making it necessary for him to develop the usual amount of male aggressiveness. Such a passive role can be exciting to a man on occasion, and he should allow himself to indulge it.

In this position the woman may straddle her husband's hips; this occasions very deep penetration, and may be particularly pleasurable because since she is in charge she may feel freer to exert more than the usual pressure of the penis against the cervix. In this position, too, she may lie on top of her husband, her legs supported by his, or she may lie between his legs. In these two latter positions the clitoris can be brought into very close contact with the penis, and this is of course very pleasant for women who become aroused in this fashion.

Another alternative for love-making is the face to face and sideways position. In this position, since the woman is generally the lighter of the two, one of her legs is placed over the man's hips; this allows him to insert his penis at a slightly oblique angle. Pillows for head and shoulder are generally necessary if this position is maintained for the entire intercourse.

The next position is the dorso-ventral position, in which

the man's penis enters the woman's vagina from the back. If the entire intercourse is performed while lying sideways, this is perhaps the most "restful" of all positions. For obvious reasons it is sometimes the preferred form for intercourse during pregnancy.

This position is often extremely exciting to a man. I do not know exactly why this is so, though it has been suggested that the position suggests the "animality" of pure lust. And this idea could be stimulated by the fact that the position is the familiar one that animals take. Or perhaps the fact that the partners are not face to face may remove some of the personal factor from the sexual embrace, giving it a more primordial and impersonal character. This may be the reason men may find it more enjoyable than women, their sexual natures being, as we have seen, somewhat more deeply rooted in their biology than the woman's sexual nature. I must emphasize, however, that these ideas are merely speculative.

The dorso-ventral position can also be assumed with the woman kneeling, or standing up and bending over, supporting herself against a chair or wall with her hands. It can be achieved less athletically if the man sits on a chair and his partner sits on his lap, although this obviously allows for less movement by both.

The last general position I shall describe here is the standing position. It is a particularly arduous position for the male; he generally must bend his knees slightly to enter and must hold onto his partner's buttocks to maintain entrance.

I think these are the major sexual positions which it is relevant to know and to adopt when the mood is upon one. Most of the "hundreds" of others described in the literature of antiquity are subtle variations of these and have no particular application to the love-making a modern couple might engage in. Indeed, I think it is apparent that any excessive preoccupation with such nuances could indicate a morbidity, may be a confession that the person, far from having achieved sexual maturity, is in some profound way impotent.

There is one further point I should like to make about these positions. While men can usually have an orgasm in any position, many women, if not most, achieve it most completely and satisfyingly in one favorite position. This is perfectly consonant with full psychological and sexual maturity, and one should in no wise feel the slightest bit apologetic about it. It is absolutely advisable to make this fact known to one's partner in love. He will, of course, if you are both feeling positionally experimental, return to the position you prefer when you are ready to have your climax.

A psychiatrist is asked a wide variety of questions about sexuality by his patients. Here are some of the most frequent areas about which individuals seem to wish further information:

(1) *Frequency of intercourse*

There are no rules whatever about this, though suggestions about what is "normal" have been made from earliest times. Mohammed the Prophet stated that once a week was best; Martin Luther found that twice a week "does harm neither to her nor to me."

In these days of sociological studies there have of course been endless attempts to find the statistical norm for frequency of intercourse. The Margaret Sanger Research Bureau in 1933 released figures showing that, of ten thousand cases investigated, sexual intercourse occurred from one to three times per week—4 per cent had intercourse one or more times daily. Kinsey found that frequency depended greatly on the age of the husband; men between twenty-one and twenty-five showed an intercourse rate of just over three times per week; those between thirty-one and thirty-five showed a frequency rate of a little more than twice a week; those aged forty-one to forty-five had intercourse on an average of one and one half times a week; and men over fifty-six averaged less than once a week.

These studies, of course, always show wide variations in individual cases.

In my opinion frequency of intercourse is entirely an individual matter. The only criterion of any importance is that both partners feel completely satisfied with the amount of intercourse they are having. If one of the partners is dissatisfied, the subject should be open for discussion in a very frank manner. No cause for feelings of rejection by a partner should be allowed to develop in silence.

There will always be periods in which, because of exterior circumstances (pregnancy, business worries, sickness, etc.), the rate of intercourse in any marriage may slow down or stop for a while.

(2) *Variations in woman's sexual desire*

There are such variations, as far as most of the research undertaken so far can determine. Katherine Davis, in a study of one thousand married women, and studies by Marie Stokes, Therese Benedek, and others indicate that the desire of women vary during the menstrual cycle. According to Hannah and Abraham Stone, who have made a study of a large number of women, "Most . . . state that their erotic impulses are increased either a few days before the onset of the menstrual flow or, more usually, right after menstruation, although the latter rise may be partly due to the abstinence which is generally maintained during the menstrual week." Stokes reported also a second rise of sexual desire at some point in the middle of the menstrual month. There are apparently individual differences in the cycle of desire, and a woman can best determine for herself her own particular rhythm.

There is much to be learned about this matter. The relationship between hormonal secretion and female sexuality and "femininity" has been most recently studied by Therese Benedek in her book *Psychosexual Functions in Women*. This is a technical book, but anyone interested in this aspect of the subject will find the material fascinating.

As far as can be determined, there is no corresponding cycle of desire in the male.

(4) *Limits to love-making*

This is entirely an individual matter. It varies with each couple and often with each intercourse. Indeed, this variability in time can add to the spontaneity factor in intercourse.

There seems to be only one basic rule governing the length of time; to see that the other partner achieves orgasm if it is desired. This often means that the husband must postpone his climax until the wife achieves hers. Most men are able to learn to control the moment at which they reach orgasm and therefore can wait until their wives are ready.

Orgasm in unison is widely held to be the most desirable form of climax. However, I have had many people of both sexes report that they preferred to reach climax immediately before or immediately after their partners. Some say that they are distracted by the other's movements at this juncture. Others say that they profoundly enjoy the partner's excitement and that they prefer to have a modicum of ego left to experience it more completely.

Some women have two or more orgasms to their husband's one. By far the majority of men have only one orgasm per intercourse. If on occasion a man has his ejaculation before the woman achieves her climax, she will often continue her movements until she is satisfied. However, the glans penis (head of the penis) of many men becomes extremely sensitive immediately after orgasm, and in that case the woman may have to postpone her satisfaction until the next time. If she continues her movements it may cause her husband to have unpleasant sensations, even though he may still have an erection and thus appear to be able to continue.

(4) *Limits to love-making*

I am often asked the question whether any sexual practice between husband and wife could be considered "unhealthy" or "wrong." In my opinion, certain practices could be considered so, though I know I am at variance with certain sexologists. A long discussion of the matter, however, would take us into psychological and even perhaps moral realms which I do not feel are pertinent to this book. As a rule of thumb, I would say that any practice that does not culminate in intercourse tends to be regressive and infantile if it becomes a chief method of sexual expression. Also, insistence on any practice that cannot be shared pleasurably by the partner is likewise regressive.

The so-called "polymorphus perverse" pleasures are aspects of foreplay and not ends in themselves. The primacy of the oral, anal, onanistic, or sado-masochistic forms of sexuality is a hallmark of the immature personality. Another unmistakable sign of such immaturity (or even of downright psychic illness) is the insistence on *any* form of sexuality not heartily endorsed by one's partner.

(5) *Contraception*

To use or not to use contraceptives is a personal matter that every individual must settle for himself.

When the responsibility for contraception is up to the woman, she should always be prepared for intercourse whenever it is even remotely possible. There is nothing so deadening to sexual excitement as the woman who comes to love unprepared and must interrupt the process to put her diaphragm on. If this is a repetitive situation in marital life it is almost a certain sign that the woman has not yet accepted her feminine role. The tacit assumption when you obtain a diaphragm is that you are accepting the responsibility for contraception. There is rarely any need, other than a negative one on the woman's part, for this to interfere or to impinge on sexual intercourse in any manner. The husband is quite correct who interprets chronic remissiveness of this sort as an unsolved problem of his wife.

ADDENDA I

Many women will find that with the methods prescribed here their frigidity can be conquered. Some, however, will find that though they can be helped by using these techniques they cannot achieve their goal without outside help. Throughout the book I have tried to indicate the kind of person and the kind of problem that may require additional therapeutic aid, and I have tried to indicate that a person who needs such outside help should feel no sense of shame about that fact nor hesitancy about seeking it. Indeed, one of my chief reasons for writing this book has been to open vistas hitherto unknown to many women. If reading it has but started you on the road to mature femininity, its chief function has been accomplished.

How does one decide whether outside aid is indicated?

There is no rule of thumb that will cover all cases. Some may decide that they would prefer to start and finish their work on this problem with a trained therapist. Others may start alone but find that self-exploration, the surfacing of painful emotions and attitudes and fantasies, is too difficult and confusing and decide to seek expert guidance. Still others may find that though they can go a long distance alone the final goal will elude them if they do not consult with a trained worker in the field.

If and when one does decide that outside help is necessary, one should know how to find qualified people in this field. The following information, then, is proffered to aid you in that respect.

Your family physician can be most helpful. If he has the time he may be able to counsel you directly, act as a guide to those insights that will help you to achieve your goal. More than likely, however, you will find that his schedule is far too heavy to permit him to do this, no matter how much he would wish to do so. In that case he will refer you to another person who is qualified to give such help or to a proper agency.

If for any reason you cannot obtain a referral from your own physician, it is important to know to whom you may turn for help in your community.

There are three kinds of specialists who are trained to give you proper counseling for your problem. These are psychiatrists, clinical psychologists, and social workers.

The hospital in your community can usually give you the name of a person in one of these specialties whom you could consult privately. Such hospitals may also have out-patient counseling clinics, and these are staffed by competent psychotherapists. If your hospital does not maintain such a service it will nevertheless know where you can obtain help.

One of the resources you have open to you may be one of the so-called "family agencies." You can have confidence in such agencies. They are devoted to the task of resolving any and all types of family problems and are frequently staffed by social workers with excellent training in marriage counseling.

Many American communities are relatively rich in counseling resources, but there are also many where psychological help is difficult to obtain. If your doctor or your local hospital cannot help you, it may be necessary for you to journey to the nearest large city to obtain aid. If you wish to obtain the names of the qualified psychiatrists nearest your residence you may write to the American Psychiatric Association, 1270 Sixth Avenue, New York, N.Y., and they will furnish you with the required information. Be certain that in your letter you specify the urban center nearest you.

ADDENDA II

There is no book that covers the problem of psychological frigidity in women as such. However, the books listed below may be helpful adjuncts to a thorough understanding of the problem. I have divided them into two categories, popular and technical.

The popular books can be understood by all. The technical books I list are generally used by physicians, but much in them can be understood by the intelligent layman.

POPULAR

The Art of Loving, Erich Fromm (New York: Harper, 1956).

A Marriage Manual, Hannah and Abraham Stone (New York: Simon and Schuster, 1952).

Modern Woman—The Lost Sex, Lundberg and Farnham (New York: Harper, 1947).

Marriage, Morals and Sex in America, Sidney Ditzion (New York: Bookman Associates, 1953).

Psychology of Sex Relations, Theodor Reik (New York: Rinehart, 1945).

The Christian Interpretation of Sex, Otto Piper (New York: Scribner, 1941).

TECHNICAL

Factors in the Sex Life of Twenty-Two Hundred Women, K. B. Davis (New York: Harper, 1929).

Female Sexuality, Marie Bonaparte (New York: International Universities Press, 1953).

The Psychology of Women (Vols. 1 and 2), Helen Deutsch (New York: Grune and Stratton, 1944-45).

Psychosexual Functions in Women, Therese Benedek (New York: Ronald Press, 1952).